CHURCH ON EDGE?

CHURCH ON EDGE?

Practising Ministry Today

John B. Thomson

DARTON · LONGMAN + TODD

First published in 2004 by
Darton, Longman and Todd Ltd
1 Spencer Court
140-142 Wandsworth High Street
London SW18 4JJ

ISBN 0-232-52566-8

A catalogue record for this book is available from the British Library.

Phototypeset by Intype Libra Ltd
Printed and bound in Great Britain by
Page Bros, Norwich, Norfolk

Contents

Acknowledgements

Stories contextualise us, they web us together. What I have written reflects this webbing and includes more than can be named. However, in particular I wish to thank Stanley Hauerwas for investing so much time and creative energy in enabling people like me to see more clearly. I wish to thank the many Africans whose exuberance for God and sacrifice have shown me other ways of imagining the love of God in Christ, thereby freeing me from captivity to an Anglocentric view of God, the church and the world. I wish to thank the parishioners of St Mary's Wheatley, Doncaster, who educated me in the surprises of discipleship in a strange place. I wish to thank my mother and late father whose exploration of Christian pilgrimage gave me the privilege of being formed as a stranger in Africa, Scotland and England. Above all I want to thank the three women of my life, Sue my wife, Anya and Emily my daughters, who have to live with the restlessness of someone who is never wholly at home!

Introduction

Since travelling to Uganda in East Africa at the age of five months, much of my life has been spent sitting on margins. As an expatriate in Africa I was marginal to the societies which had inhabited this area for centuries. When we visited Britain we were aware of being on the edge, particularly at local schools, because of our heritage, our accents and the different customs we observed. I was twelve when my family returned to reside in the United Kingdom, and the sense of being on the edge of life intensified as five years of moving around England and Scotland and the memory of an African childhood combined to locate us as strangers in most contexts we found ourselves in. Perhaps this was why the idea of spending part of my theological education in another country, South Africa, was so appealing. However, a subsequent period of three years' teaching there reinforced the sense of being an alien, since as a white in the era of transition from apartheid my body symbolised the pain of history, thereby marginalising my contribution to the way the Christian community was negotiating this period of change. Returning to England and to an incumbency in inner urban Doncaster in South Yorkshire located me in the very alien context of predominantly working-class communities. Again I found myself as an outsider trying to understand and enter a Christian conversation with folk remarkably different to myself and to the norms I assumed.

I am deeply grateful for all of this, disturbing and de-centring as it has been, since I have become increasingly convinced that the margins and edge are where God is inviting Christian people to be in the sort of societies emerging in the so-called 'west'. Such an experience is profoundly traumatic, particularly for those whose hopes and dreams are bound up with being significant and in publicly recognised power. Some have called this the demise of the Constantinian project, whose roots go back to the emperor Constantine's decision to become a Christian in the fourth century, thereby making the Christian faith the religion of the Roman Empire. I am not sure to what extent this demise has happened, though I do agree that much has changed as the politics of our society have disengaged from the practices of public worship and prayer. However as a practising Christian and priest, my concern here is not to try to offer a speculative assessment of English society, but to explore how being church in this sort of society asks of us an imaginative and devotional journey which is helped by seeing things through the lens of liminality.

In reflecting this way I am trying to do theology in conversational mode, that is, as an act of prayerful reflection upon how a particular journey has shaped the way God can be seen to be acting in the sort of society we are becoming. As such this is more biographical and colloquial than some would feel appropriate. However, if theology is to speak it must be in 'parole' rather than in 'langue', it must be about dialect rather than 'the Queen's English', it must be about bringing what our journey evokes and sharing this rather than trying to represent a universal story.

This short book is therefore a meditation upon a journey, inviting fellow travellers to share their own narratives and hoping to stimulate imaginative ways of taking the next step with God in Christ. There are many stimulating books on ways of developing congregations, improving the way churches go about their business and suggesting models and activities which can address the urgent challenge of congregational decline. I do not presume that this book can add much to these in the first instance. However, behind this book lies the shadow of the theological ethicist, Stanley Hauerwas, who taught me the importance of attending first to who we should be in God's kingdom before deciding what we should do; of becoming aware of our distinctive character as practising Christians before we rush around trying to resolve the problems of an institution or indeed of the world. In short we have to be trained to see who and what we are in God's redeeming community. Looking from the edges and having been formed as someone living on a variety of edges, I simply seek to share what I see and the way this sort of view can offer resources of hope for the Christian community in England at this time. If this helps others to see themselves and their situations in new and creative ways then I rejoice.

1 Feeling edgy

Recovering the ordinary

'Why can't we see ordinary people like us?' was the response from a mixed group of adults preparing for confirmation. I had shown them a video, which represented four superficially ordinary people from inner urban churches in one of our great northern cities who had come to faith as adults. However, each of them had a 'mega-testimony' which spoke of Christ rescuing them from such legacies as family breakdown, alcoholism or the occult. Yet to these confirmands the people on screen were no longer ordinary, but extraordinary. Their redemption was from something remarkable and challenging. Certainly those gathered had problems and challenges themselves but they were not in the same league. Hence they felt alienated by the very attempt to portray ordinary people finding God at work in their lives. Paradoxically the 'interest' value of these exemplars made them relative celebrities and hence distant from the sort of people being drawn to ask what God might mean in their lives in a relatively mundane parish in Doncaster.

Celebrity culture infuses everything in late modern western societies, dominated as they are by the visual media. All is about the eye and about being noticed and, while so-called 'reality TV' presents itself in programmes such as *Big Brother* or *Pop Idol* as about ordinary people, it actually trades on the hunger for notoriety which is but another name for celebrity. As soon as people participate, they enter a controlled and highly artificial environment, which is driven by the need to form people into celebrities whose identities can be aspired to but not generalised. The whole agenda is to use the ordinary as a backcloth and reservoir from which celebrities escape, rather than to offer the remaining ordinary a sense of their own value and significance.

In the pursuit of excellence, this has always been the case, as music and sport, the university and crafts display. Indeed there is nothing intrinsically wrong with this, though *Big Brother* could never seriously be categorised as about the pursuit of excellence. Where it becomes corrosive is when this pursuit assumes an all-consuming and all-pervasive character. This then diminishes the very life it depends upon, which is the primary value of ordinary people in ordinary life, whose own character is underplayed, under-appreciated, and who thereby become disempowered in the face of such an all-powerful prescription of significance. What my confirmation group were rebelling against was the unrecognised extension of this into a well-meaning video about transformed lives. These lives represented ironic celebrity, since the very pathologies they portrayed indicated a noteworthiness which marginalised the experience of the confirmands. The latter felt that their stories represented too mundane a reality to be of note. If the real divine action was in such people as those on the video, then their own lives were certainly second best.

The confirmands may have been overreactive. After all, celebrities such as monarchs, courtiers and even bishops have been with us in England for centuries. Indeed without some attention to the special, life would be very dull. It seems no accident that societies which sought to establish a level playing field, in the great twentieth-century experiment of state socialism, simply achieved dullness for the majority and, in certain cases, a hypocritical life for the elite. We need transcendence. Nevertheless, just as state-determined egalitarianism destroyed its people's vitality, so celebrity culture is destroying ours. Indeed, in some ways, in spite of superficial differences, celebrity culture is as dull as its socialist antithesis, since it manufactures clones as effectively as the egalitarians. It offers elitist and monochrome transcendence. The only difference is that the clones are set apart on a pedestal from the majority rather than being the majority. They function as the social stereotypes, thereby reducing the rainbow character of those dazzled by their white light.

Late western modernity is a culture devoted to pastiche and image. It is about virtual reality as opposed to embodiment, imaged ideals as opposed to the messy details of difference. Inevitably this infuses the Christian community as it breathes in the cultural air of its context. Where this is particularly evident is in the celebrity cults prevalent among the evangelical wing of the church, my own pedigree. Despite its rhetorical commitment in matters of religion to simplicity, accessibility and egalitarianism, the story of recent evangelicalism has inclined towards an uncritical colonisation by celebrity culture in a way analogous to its earlier uncritical espousal of much of the legacy of Enlightenment rationalism. Both reflect the hunger for relevance which informs evangelicals' passion to share the Gospel in ways intelligible to those among whom they live.

Indeed this was no doubt why I had unconsciously selected this video and was surprised by the reaction of those watching it. In the quest to indicate how the transcendence of God was present in others superficially like my confirmation group, I had actually bought into the cultural stream of celebrity. This evoked the rebellion of the group who could not recognise analogous transcendence in their own lives. What they were asking of me as their priest was for a theology of the ordinary, which could illuminate and nourish the mundane realities of parish life and congregational discipleship. Given that most parishes in the Church of England, and, I suspect, most church communities of other Christian traditions, face this challenge, I found myself needing to explore what resources were available to help such ordinary Christian people see their stories and identities as vital and significant contributions to, and participations in, the great epic of God's cosmic engagement with creation.

Recovering the church

When in 1988 at the National Evangelical Anglican Congress the late Archbishop Robert Runcie challenged evangelicals in the Church of England about the adequacy of their doctrine of church, I remember thinking that he had put his finger on a very important issue. At the time I was not able to engage with the challenge creatively, but it struck me that this identified a vulnerability within the tradition which had formed me whose corrosive contribution to the demise of church in our society was underestimated. To regard the Church of England as simply the best boat to fish from implied a utilitarian and instrumental view of a church, which could be replaced if a more effective utility came along and which had no intrinsic contribution to the identity of those within it. The church was simply a pretext for the more fundamental notion of salvation as a voluntary and essentially individualistic experience, shared with others of like experience, but not dependent in character upon more than their testimony. In addition, 'church' under this form was simply a contemporary community able to gain immediate access to its foundational testimonies in the Bible without being webbed into the intervening church. At best the latter were story sharers. At worst they were a dispensable nuisance.

Furthermore, a tendency among evangelicals to sectarianism both within the Church of England and beyond it raised concerns in an increasingly consumerist and voluntarist society. Unless a more robust ecclesiology emerged, evangelical congregations would represent church clubs and thereby be open to corrosion by the acidic tendencies of voluntarism and consumerism. Clubs are groups of people who voluntarily contract into a collective, which provides certain goods sought for and hence is vulnerable to disengagement if the contract is perceived to be inadequate. Church clubs, paradoxically, also open the way to dictatorship, since the absence of intrinsic bonds means that external policing becomes the most secure way of ensuring social order. Hence there are two tendencies evident in the evangelical tradition. On the one hand there are many evangelicals who 'shop' around, for the best church, the church which best suits their dispositions as consumers. On the other hand successful evangelical churches have a tendency to adulate the strong leader or leadership team and seek considerable structural accountability and coherence within the congregation.

My experience as an assistant minister in a suburban church struggling to represent an open evangelical tradition which did not ignore its parochial calling focused the problem acutely for me. The very strengths we represented were the occasions of our swiftest losses. By sharing the Gospel in ways which emphasised individual response to a conscious experience of divine grace within a community seeking to explore worship more passionately and fellowship more intimately, we produced the very sort of Christians whose eyes and hearts would be drawn to better examples of the same in our locality. Since the essentials of discipleship were located in the individual believer, the church became a secondary reality whose role was to enable that individual to flourish in faith. If that flourishing appeared more likely in another church, then the priority was to move to where life seemed to be. Commitment to a particular community of faith in a certain context was not intrinsic to the identity of those being grafted into this church. Indeed to the most committed the parish context was, in many ways, a relative drag on the church's resources of time, place and energy. Certainly it provided mission and service opportunities or fishing grounds, but the identity of being church, as envisaged in the tradition of parish church, was increasingly difficult to sustain. Church was fundamentally the gathering of the committed rather than the parish complexity of wheat and tares. It was for activists rather than for a more diffuse constituency and was to sustain rather than form these activists.

It was with these ambivalences that I travelled with my wife and seven-week-old daughter to St Paul's College, Grahamstown in South Africa in response to an invitation to teach at the Anglican seminary there following the completion of my assistant role in Sheffield. I had already spent two terms of my final year as an ordinand on exchange at St Paul's, and although we were anxious about relocating to a country in the throes of the apartheid conflict, we felt that if this was of God then it should be explored. As it happened every obstacle we anticipated disappeared and we arrived on Steve Biko Day, 12 September 1989.

Over the next three years the church in South Africa offered me a twofold theological challenge. The first was to reflect upon what it meant to be part of a community formed from within the catholic tradition of Anglicanism. St Paul's had its pedigree in the missionary service of the College of the Resurrection, Mirfield, West Yorkshire, and this exposed me to the practices of a tradition committed to notions of ecclesial formation which I had never encountered and probably would have avoided if I had remained in England. In short it provided me with an adventure in exploring what being church might mean not as a fishing vessel or as a club of activists, but as a society within and through which discipleship is practised.

The second was liberation theology or southern theology, which directly challenged the ways I had learned theology in England. Liberation theology challenged the western tradition's claims to universal currency and, in particular, challenged evangelicalism's apparent privatisation of faith through its focus upon the abstract and pietistic individual. Instead of being part of the vanguard church, liberation theology represented the evangelicalism of my heritage as part of the problem rather than the solution. Whether it be African, black, feminist, Latin American or even Afrikaner theology, the message was the same. To be white, male, educated in the western tradition, evangelical, a priest of a colonising church and representative of a colonising country and culture was to be a problem.

These twin influences, fused together in the painful and de-centring socio-political changes of South Africa, provided the crucible within which was forged my own hesitant response to the questions haunting me. Over the three years we were in the country I sought to engage openly and actively with these streams of 'otherness', increasingly aware not only of my own superficial theological awareness but also of the way these streams questioned whether the evangelical stream in the Church of England was adequately church.

The fragile character of theological education and the uncertainties of the future in South Africa added intensity to these reflections. There was no certainty that there was much time or place for what I represented either in St Paul's or, indeed, in the sort of church that the Church of the Province was becoming as the socio-economic experiment of apartheid was deposed. In addition, the particular challenges of living in a non-racial community within a racist society demanded considerable energies and education as the anger and pain of ordinands, who represented the victims of apartheid, surfaced. What this did, however, was to distil in me a number of questions which I brought back to England when St Paul's was closed and a new college, the College of the Transfiguration, formed from it and its fellow seminary, St Bede's. These questions revolved around the kind of church appropriate to the context of late modern society in England and, in a relatively underdeveloped way, I regarded my first living as an experiment in what it might be to be church in a context where the challenges were acute, namely in South Yorkshire and, in particular, in an inner urban parish.

What the church in South Africa had helped me to grasp was

that discipleship is intrinsically integrated with being church as a social and liberating order particularly among the marginalised. Yet it had equally indicated to me that being church had to take account of the messiness and details of itself and its context. Ideal churches do not exist, nor do 'ahistorical' churches. Whatever the strengths of evangelical witness in the context of modernity, the challenge I faced was how to practise a more embodied, as opposed to rhetorical, apologetic of Christian liberty. I was beginning to grasp that the primary agency of the Gospel was not the abstract individual, but the church as an embodied community extending through time and across the globe. Where as a youngster I had been led to believe that the individual was the focus of attention, I was now coming to the view that the church must be the focus of attention. In short I was becoming a more catholic evangelical.

Hence in approaching my first incumbency I was excited by the challenge of exploring how the Gospel could be embodied in the life and service of a community in an area on the margins of church possibility. How might the church in this superficially barren environment display the presence of the light of Christ in and for the people living around it? In an odd sort of way this integrated the earlier tributaries of a childhood in Uganda and early adolescence in Scotland within the explorations I was engaged with. Those experiences had led to the conviction that the international church was an essential conversation partner for the church in England if we were truthfully and properly to grasp our vocation. After South Africa I could now see that this was not simply an auxiliary role, but an intrinsic one.

Our eight years at St Mary's once again became a profoundly challenging yet creative experience. I remember visiting the local shops during my first few weeks as vicar to introduce myself. One of the shopkeepers was an Afro-Caribbean woman whose response to my greeting both shocked and sobered me. She had neither warmth nor humour and her reaction had a degree of hostility in it which I had not met even in the agonies of South Africa. If I had learned that in South Africa, as a descendant of the British Empire, I had four hundred years of history on my back, I learned that as vicar of this parish I had about nineteen hundred years of church history on my back, some of which was infused with the racism of the recent forty years represented in the reactive anger of this Afro-Caribbean newsagent. To be church in this area was going to involve accepting the presence of this past in every encounter. The Gospel would have to be a Gospel which recognised the history of the context in all its webbed character.

Furthermore it soon became clear to me that the limited commitment of local white people to the practice of being church was due less to the impact of the choice culture of late modernity and more to do with practices reaching back into the distant past of urbanisation and the role of the Church of England in the past, as representative of the powerful. As one elderly widow mentioned to me, when she was a girl during the interwar period, her sort were not allowed to call at the vicarage front door. Instead the side door was reserved for such as her. Romantic notions of an easy embrace of a liberating Gospel were shattered by the depth memory of a church representing a 'gospel' of exclusion and social hierarchy. Equally, attempts to engage with local people through the individualistic emphasis of evangelical evangelism were met with equal ambivalence by the predominantly artisan and working-class locals. Certainly some did become part of the congregation through direct challenge. However, these folk were predominantly people who had moved into the area rather than those who represented the more settled communities.

Such responses, together with the questions that were still with me from South Africa and before, led me to grapple further with the character of church in conversation with the American theological ethicist, Stanley M. Hauerwas. The academic consequence of this was that I wrote a PhD on his work.[1] The more significant consequence was that a symbiotic relationship developed between my ministerial practices in this inner urban parish and my reflective practices as student. Together these began to give shape to an understanding of what church might mean as the legacy of this history and the implications of late modernity enriched my evangelical heritage.

Recovering the Bible?

The third troubling question that has occupied me over the years is one which emerged from a challenge Professor Ernest Nicholson gave to those of us gathered in the chapel of Wycliffe Hall, Oxford, when I was an ordinand there in the early 1980s. Professor Nicholson, if I recall correctly, was on the Council of Wycliffe Hall at the time and therefore a friend of the broadly evangelical tradition, which Wycliffe represented. He is an Old Testament biblical scholar of note. It was for these reasons that his challenge given during a chapel sermon was so acute. As I remember he said something akin to 'make sure that you, as evangelicals, actually read the Bible!' To folk convinced that our evangelical pedigree was secure, this seemed like challenging the French to ensure that they spoke French.

Yet upon reflection and as a result of theological studies, teaching and, in particular, parish ministry, I have increasingly felt the force of this challenge. Nicholson was challenging us to attend to the primacy of the Scriptures rather than reading the Scriptures through some anterior ideological lens. Such attention reveals that the character of Scripture, its socio-historical location and its role, are more complex and demanding than is often evident, certainly in more populist evangelical writings. Indeed, as many others have commented, much populist evangelical hermeneutics represents a smuggled and undeclared 'common-sense' philosophical tradition more at home in modernist and rationalist circles than in the world of Scripture itself. Similarly the individualistic emphasis, given substance by the notion of the perspicuity of Scripture, fails to recognise the dangers of self-deception and the social character of identity and interpretation.

Hence the very attractive qualities of the evangelical tradition, with its stress on the primacy of Scripture, the accessibility of Scripture, the clarity of Scripture, could render the reading of Scripture prey to an unrecognised or undeclared pretext either of common-sense Enlightenment philosophy or an anterior and timeless ideology whose truth was underwritten by extensive and often arbitrary selection of scriptural quotations. Both in England and in South Africa I increasingly found that this approach denuded the Scriptures of their intrinsic identity as a series of stories about God's engagement with creation and in particular his people over several millennia, a story still ongoing and drawing towards its climax in the Parousia or second advent of Christ.

While the character and status of the Bible as Scripture

occupied me as an assistant priest seeking to engage with the questions of parishioners faced with a society increasingly ambivalent about the capacity of these Scriptures to deliver, it was once again the impact of reading the Bible in the southern African context which opened up many issues which I had not been introduced to in my Christian formation to date. Issues of context, hermeneutics, the role of readers, the place of church, corrupt and genuine readings and the place of the marginal in the distillation of scriptural truth were all forced upon me by the way the Bible was being explored by Christians under very different conditions from those I had engaged with in England. In addition, this was an approach unwilling to accept what it regarded as a pietistic reduction of the resources of Scripture evident in the more evangelical traditions. Scripture was not simply a solution to personal salvation and holiness, but a resource to challenge the powers that seek to rule in a way antagonistic to God's reign.

In essence the Bible suddenly expanded into a drama of cosmic proportions, which offered critical resources for resistance and liberty for those suffering the fallout from such pretentious ruling. Protagonists of liberation theology, in particular, found new ways of reading the Bible, which sought to escape from the expertise of the academy and to engage ordinary Christian readers in contexts quite alien to the security of university campuses. At the same time Africans were revisiting the Scriptures as they grappled with what it might mean to be an African church rather than a pale imitation of the Church of England. Issues of circumcision, naming ceremonies, the place of ancestors in contemporary life, traditional healings and the like were refracted through the Scriptures using African eyes as opposed to European ones. Jesus was seen as closer in spirit to much of black African practice than to the practices inherited from Europe, especially Britain, through the missionaries.

These approaches to reading Scripture in context not only contributed to a de-centring of myself as 'expert' biblical teacher or theologian, but challenged me to revisit the Scriptures in conversation with ordinary, marginal people. Without denying the wisdom of much that had been given to me through ministerial formation and theological education, this southern challenge asked of me questions of power as well as insight when engaging in scriptural exegesis. Was I sufficiently aware of the character and complexity of my identity as 'I' engaged in this exegesis? Was I sufficiently in conscious conversation with enough partners to limit the prejudices and blindness I was as yet unaware of? Was I actively seeking out the church as a community committed to exploring the Bible as Scripture together, or did I see myself as a singular interpreter offering a singular interpretation of the Scriptures, which needed no assistance to be discerned? In short, had I appreciated the social character of the 'I' that I am and sought to become more aware of the assets and liabilities of this social ego?

Having said this, I was also increasingly aware that most liberation theology in the southern African context was still generated by theologians within the academy. Much theology and biblical studies in congregations seemed to remain at the level of either common-sense philosophy or paternalistic dictatorship, a situation not aided by the terrible legacy of 'Bantu education'. Hence, though convinced that the insights of the academy were pertinent, the first challenge for me was to see whether they offered a more truthful attention to Scripture in an ordinary church. The second, in the light of this, was to explore what the relationship of a church in an ordinary parish in England to Scripture might entail.

However, upon taking up the role of vicar of St Mary's Wheatley, Doncaster, in 1993 I became aware that a simple reiteration of the insights and themes which had so challenged me in South Africa could not be done. In the first place, they could not simply be transferred across such swathes of space and time. The rhetoric and the contexts were so different that it would be easy to alienate people by giving the impression that truth was to be received from elsewhere, a pathology which was the very one the liberation theologians were seeking to challenge in their own context. Second, there was the danger of proffering an abstract idealistic view of the Bible, as with the church, which took no account of how local reading and tradition informed interpretation. If the Bible was a fundamental resource for a living community whose embodiments were in distinctive contexts, then to read the Bible as if the particular histories and contexts of a given interpretative community did not matter was to undermine the place of the Bible in the Christian community's life. This would be to return to the very error I felt I had had to grapple with in earlier days.

The way I tentatively explored this approach to the Bible was reinforced through my engagement with the theological ethics of Stanley Hauerwas as mentioned above. Hauerwas, it seemed to me, was attempting to explore the social 'I' through his ecclesial ethics. As such, for Hauerwas the Scriptures belong within the interpretative community of the church through and across time and space, since it is this community which identifies them as its Scriptures and seeks its identity as a people worshipping the God of Jesus Christ through the memory of God's ways with Israel, the Jews, Jesus and the early church.[2] What Hauerwas was offering me, as will be apparent below, was a way of connecting Scripture and church that offered space for the insights of liberation theologians about the marginalised as readers, but also a way of speaking of the particular attentions that distinctive embodiments of church have for the Scriptures. In essence, the local congregation, in conversation with the wider church, past and present, is a primary interpreter of Scripture with biblical scholars, theologians and others as assistants rather than arbiters of that interpretation. Here, it seemed to me, was a possible response to Ernest Nicholson's challenge to ensure that the Bible was actually being read truthfully and properly.

Summary

Three ecclesial concerns emerged as I grappled with my formation as a Christian within the broadly evangelical expression of Anglicanism, each one touching a core intention of the evangelical agenda: God's passion for the ordinary person; the importance of personal salvation; and the primacy of the Bible as Scripture. Paradoxically, under the pressure of modernity and now late modernity, these very laudable intentions were actually delivering their opposite. First, in the quest to reach ordinary people in a 'relevant' way they were actually leading to the edging out of the ordinary in preference to the celebrity and the expert. Second, the church was being edged out as the language of personhood was equated with individualism and freedom interpreted in voluntarist terms. Third, the Bible was being edged out, as a failure to appreciate sufficiently the integration of community and text in the hermeneutical endeavour had led to an approach which disempowered ordinary Christians and left the Bible in the hands of a new 'clerical' elite or unexamined cultural assumptions.

This book, therefore, represents the explorations of a 'catholic' evangelical mediated through the practice of ministry over 17 years in South Yorkshire and South Africa. It reflects a search for the body of Christ in discipleship and ministry in the conviction that this body is intrinsic to the possibility of the latter. It is an exploration of the marginal location of this body in the perceptions of much contemporary English society. In so doing I am reminded of the story of Abram and Lot, where the promise is not to be found in the green fields of Sodom but on the liminal heights of Canaan.[3] The mystery of God's ways with the world and the church seem somehow to be about being edged out, decentred, away from where superficial significance and relevance are to be found. The green hill outside a city wall is where the real action takes place.

Yet it is on the margins or edges that we can see the unexpected and surprising. Margins indicate what is really valuable and enable us to celebrate costly but creative living. I once led a service with a small congregation of evangelical pedigree in a deprived area of south-west Barnsley. There were fifteen adults and two children in the congregation, all bar two of the adults were women, and all bar two were over fifty. In the middle of the sermon, four young lads burst in through the door. I could tell that the women knew these kids and had mixed feelings about their presence, but they invited them in, sat them down at the front of the church and the lads stayed for the rest of the service and received a blessing. During the sermon, whose theme was 'God can make tombs into wombs', I asked 'what's still left open in this area?' and the reply was 'the shop, the chippy and the church'. The pub and many of the houses around were empty and boarded up. The shop and chippy were there because they had an economic interest in staying open. The church was open because of God's interest in sharing his life through this fragile faithful community. In the most rugged of soils a church was alive and able to welcome the marginalised as a marginal community witnessing to a marginalised God. Here was an example of 'catholic' evangelicals in action and this book is dedicated to such communities whose witness most faithfully tells the story of Immanuel, God-with-us.

2 Marginal speech

Feeling tongue-tied

When we first moved to Doncaster our younger daughter, Emily, was about eighteen months old. As is customary, the local health visitor undertook a number of health checks, including a hearing test. The latter involved asking the child to perform certain tasks and I remember Emily being asked to pass a duck over to the visitor. However, when asked to do this Emily didn't respond. When asked a second time, again she didn't respond. It was only when the health visitor pointed to the duck that she passed it over with a shy yet bemused smile. The health visitor expressed some concern about this and indicated to us that there might be a hearing impairment, which should be further explored by a consultant at the Doncaster Royal Infirmary. We ourselves were somewhat perplexed, since we had never noticed any hearing problems when speaking to Emily. Instead we believed that Emily didn't understand the command since it was given in broad Doncaster English rather than in a South African dialect or our own dialects with which she was familiar. In short it was not her hearing that was at fault but her language skills. She could not hear or speak Doncaster English. She had not been formed in this part of the English-speaking world. Our diagnosis was confirmed when Sue, my wife, took her to see the consultant and, after the appropriate tests were done at the hospital, Emily was declared to possess perfect hearing.

Emily's experience represents a parable of what has been happening to the Christian church in England and much of the western world during the post-war period. We worry that the language we took for granted as the means by which the Gospel was shared no longer enables us to communicate. We think that dissonance rather than harmony is now the norm. It's as if we have become the health visitor addressing a new patient and finding that this patient no longer understands the dialect or language we are speaking. Furthermore, having found that folk around us no longer immediately understand what we are on about, we have lost confidence in the language we speak. Hence the pressure has been upon us to forget the place and character of our mother tongue as Christians and try to represent our truth and reality claims in the language which calls itself neutral 'secular discourse'.

In responding this way we have implicitly accepted the assumption that there is a universal language by which reality is mediated, called 'secular discourse'. Furthermore this discourse seems to position and contain our Christian language within its presumed totality. Secular discourse appears not to need such religious language to make sense of the world for all serious purposes. Rather it tolerates and polices such language much as it tolerates and polices folk who wish to use a sport or other enthusiasm as a way of giving metaphorical colour to 'bread-and-butter reality'. Religious and thus Christian discourse is an aesthetic add-on which is easily disposed of when no longer required. It can be translated into a more adequate language without remainder. It can be reduced to something else without fundamental loss to its currency. It is essentially soluble.

Such a marginalising and reductive tactic is evident not only among Christianity's cultured despisers, but also among western Christians seeking to be relevant to the world they are in. Hearing the frequently repeated assertion that this is a secular age and society, Christians feel compelled to re-present the Christian story in the 'language' of their hearers. Indeed, in some sense, this is felt to be faithful to the character of the New Testament, which employed *koine* Greek to mediate the story of the Messiah to a non-Jewish world. Yet the key question this sort of approach evokes is whether the media overwhelms the message or remains subservient to it. For, in the quest to be relevant, all can be lost if the agenda of the sharer is set by a way of framing life which itself is antagonistic to that agenda. To use another analogy, the question for any second-language speaker is whether he or she retains confidence in the worthiness of their primary language even as they find themselves using another tongue to convey what they wish to share.

Recovering our fluency

It is this issue of confidence in our mother tongue and what it means to be relevant which occupies many of us called to be church today. As mentioned in the last chapter, a passion among evangelicals is to enable ordinary folk to receive the Gospel in a clear and personal manner. Yet I also noted the way celebrity culture has colonised this intention and corrupted it, as the price of relevance has been to deploy celebrity Christians as paradigms of discipleship. In the process the really ordinary people have been marginalised and their stories of faith rendered less interesting and significant. It is as if the language of celebrity, so powerful in our 'secular' society, has changed the character of the Gospel, which its employment was intended to further. In the mundane contexts of much discipleship celebrity models can appear superficially attractive but in fact simply indicate the relative poverty of their admirers. In contrast, one of the lessons I learned as a child from humble Ugandan Christians was that St Peter's description of the church in 1 Peter 2:1–10 revealed ordinary Christians to be royalty, or all celebrities, since they were part of the community of Christ the King. A similar insight emerged from liberation theologians seeing the marginal as the primary concern of God. For both, relevance to the Gospel is not about emulating the values and aspirations of dominant culture but framing life using the language of Christian believing. In short, being relevant to the Gospel is about speaking a distinctive language, which, in this case, identifies the real celebrities as the insignificant and anonymous ones of God's community, or the 'little ones' of Matthew's gospel. In England these 'little ones' comprise most of our gathered congregations, as well as those who represent the underbelly of our social order. To recognise their royalty is to articulate the language of God's grace in a way which sees in ordinary lives the glory of God and thereby subverts the corrosive effects of celebrity culture.

Recovering confidence in our mother tongue, the language of Christian believing, is therefore vital in the late modern context of English society. We need to become fluent speakers again. However, this is also difficult since by 'language' we are not speaking about rhetoric, that is, particular words alone, but about the way we construe reality in its deepest sense. We are using language as a way of distilling and declaring our convictions about the realities of existence. This is much akin to the explorations of languages in the film *Wit*. Emma Thompson plays an English professor, Vivienne, a scholar of the seventeenth-century poet John Donne, who is diagnosed with terminal cancer. The film explores the descriptive power of a number of languages, including Donne's metaphysics, technological medicine and human friendship, testing which language is more truthful in its descriptive capacities. At the start of the film it is clear that the dominant language is that of medical technology. However, the inadequacy of this language becomes increasingly evident as not only do the medical procedures bring no cure, but also this language cannot respond to the human experience of dying. Donne's poetry seems more adept at this. However, the twist is in the penultimate scene, when Vivienne's former teacher, who introduced her to Donne's sonnets, visits her as she is dying. At this point neither the language of medical technology nor indeed the recitation of Donne's Sonnets is adequate. She simply climbs onto the bed and cradles Vivienne's head in her arms while reading a book of short stories for a five-year-old. This human embrace, the first time Vivienne has received human warmth in the film, combined with her own assurance through the Christian hope of Donne, enables the teacher to give Vivienne permission to die well. The final scene, when the young registrar doctor discovers Vivienne's dead body and tries to reimpose the instrumental language of medical technology through an unwanted resuscitation, brings the contest into sharp relief. This language, so dominant in the hospital, is in fact an inadequate language to the mystery of human living and dying. Paradoxically it is at this point that the young registrar realises that he is speaking the wrong mother tongue!

For Christians in societies such as England it is not always clear when we are losing our mother tongue and being colonised by alien discourses. In addition, since, rhetorically, the language we speak seems little different to that of our neighbours, we often are unaware that what we are saying as Christians may no longer be communicating as we might imagine. Equally, the gradual way the 'secular' appears to be dislocating from its traditional sense in Christian discourse means that we are not always aware of where the boundaries are between the two and to what extent the 'secular' as a language exists as anything other than a parasite upon the more fundamental language of Christian believing. Indeed we are not even sure whether the 'secular' is actually another language, or a dialect which can be recovered for Christian discipleship. Historically 'secular' or the *saeculum* was a term used in two ways by Christians. First, it was used to identify the age between the resurrection and the second advent of Christ, when the Spirit is active but the full disclosure of God's agenda remains hidden. Second, it was used to describe the environment within which the laity exercised their divine vocation to order the politics of society while the clergy were responsible for its liturgical ordering. In both cases it was an explicitly Christian word. It is only in more recent times that it has come to represent a way of construing reality independent of Christian or indeed religious rhetoric and wisdom. Hence its somewhat ambiguous character and the lack of clarity about its capacity to transcend its pedigree without dissolving into nothingness.[1]

Untying the tongue: two examples from parish experience

Trying to negotiate and clarify this linguistic confusion is part of the challenge of being church today. In England this ambiguity is practically focused around the meaning of 'establishment' and the question of whether English society is sufficiently Christian in pedigree and practice to warrant an explicit orientation around the grammar of Christian discourse in Anglican dialect. From my experience as a vicar negotiating this ambiguity on a regular basis, two examples of this linguistic describing remain fixed in my memory, the first to do with the describing of prostitution in our area and the second to do with the describing of the Millennium celebrations.

During the last three years of my time as vicar of St Mary's Wheatley, Doncaster there was a change of police tactics regarding prostitution. What had effectively been a sort of informal tolerance around the centre of the town was now challenged with a more active attempt to disperse the prostitutes and pimps from their traditional sites. The upshot of this was that the 'problem' arrived on the streets of our parish including St Mary's Road where the parish church and the vicarage stood. Not surprisingly local people became increasingly incensed as they could no longer walk around the streets after dusk because of soliciting prostitutes or the attentions of kerb-crawlers. In addition the area was gaining an informal reputation as a 'red-light' area with consequent threats to property prices, sales and perceptions about the character of the area. For some years residents and businesses had suffered the effects of drug abuse in thefts and discarded syringes. Now prostitution was adding a further stigma to the place.

Some years before, a number of us on St Mary's Road had formed a Neighbourhood Watch and I had been elected to take the chair. During its early years the Watch was mainly concerned with security awareness in the light of the drug and thieving problems, with street lighting and, on occasion, with concerns about the number and character of multiple occupancy premises on the street. However, with the arrival of prostitutes from the town centre, St Mary's Road became a principal site for soliciting and kerb-crawling, since it formed a cut-through between two arterial roads, had some of the poorest street lighting in Doncaster at the time and had plenty of dark accessible alleyways at hand which made police surveillance very difficult. This put the Neighbourhood Watch to the test, a test which some of the locals felt we were failing, since the initial tactic of informing the police of girls on the street and taking number plates of kerb-crawlers when we saw them seemed inadequate. Direct action was sought and as a result street patrols were set up by local people and each night a group of residents would stand on the street to deter kerb-crawlers from stopping.

As vicar I was put in a difficult position, which entailed supporting residents in their attempt to rid the street of prostitutes, while at the same time attending to the issues involved in this prostitution, namely drug dependency, social exclusion and underage girls who were predominantly addicts dominated by their drug-pushing pimps. The Christian language represented both as part of God's concern, even if the way that concern should be expressed had to attend to issues of priority and possibility. Indeed it became apparent to me that we had had one or more prostitutes attending the church over the course of my time as vicar. Hence any response to the problem could not rest content with a 'not-in-my-back-yard', approach, even this was what most local residents wanted.

What did emerge, in conversation with the church and the residents, was a series of public meetings held in the church hall to which the MP, town councillors, the police and, on the second occasion, Street Reach (a local project attempting to offer help and escape to prostitutes), and the highways department of the council were invited to hear local people's concerns. Given the spread of the problem, residents from adjoining roads also attended and somewhat heated exchanges were had about police tactics, the best way forward and wider concerns about the inadequacy of the law to deal with the issues prostitution raised, particularly regarding sanctions against kerb-crawlers. I believe that it was partly as a result of these meetings that our MP, Rosie Winterton, pressed the then Home Secretary, Jack Straw, to include in the Queen's Speech of that year proposed legislation to make kerb-crawling a criminal offence.

My part in all of this was to keep the conversations going in such a way that the Christian description of the situation was present. The grammar of Christian discourse indicated that the 'strangers' of life were to be those we should seek to befriend. Hence even the prostitutes and pimps were to be included in the debates, even if it was too problematic to have them physically present. The invitation to Street Reach was an attempt to include these strangers, at least vicariously, in the conversation even though not all were sympathetic to this strategy. However, without their presence the conversation would have been inadequate from a Christian perspective. Without their presence the realities of the situation could not be truthfully described and simple self-interest might have been all that was articulated.

Interestingly this Christian grammar worked much more effectively when I was silent and other participants actively spoke. My role as priest and vicar was primarily to ensure that the conversations properly represented and thus described what was happening in Christian language. This language described the strangers represented in the prostitutes and pimps as neighbours who had to be 'loved'. Our challenge was to explore how that might happen, rather than simply press for their swift dispersal. Remarkably it was as others spoke that I heard the mother tongue of Christian believing contributing to the conversation and its outcomes through their voices.

A second example of an attempt to restore a Christian description to a significant event involved our local celebration of the Millennium. Like many others, I was concerned that public celebrations were proceeding with little significant attention to the language implicit in the calendar date. It was a classic instance of the dislocation of a particular chronology from its narrative pedigree and by implication the underplaying of the contribution of that pedigree to contemporary life. However, I felt that our local response to this should not simply be critique but active counter-testimony. We should, in short, talk up our mother tongue and invite other sympathetic folk to join with us in so doing. It was therefore with gratitude that I happened to hear of the musical *Hopes and Dreams*, a Rob Frost Team Project.[2] *Hopes and Dreams* represents an imaginative and creative rendition of the Lord's Prayer in dramatic and musical form and immediately I could see that it offered an opportunity to celebrate the Millennium in our language. Yet doing this would mean recognising the 'conjunctions' inherent in that language. These 'conjunctions' were ordinary people in our area, in particular the local schools, the Riley School of Dance, the South Yorkshire Crusade Choir as well as Wheatley Churches Together, our local ecumenical partnership. To speak the Millennium in Christian discourse was about inviting others to share in the occasion. It was to be hospitable in eucharistic mode.

The result of this was three most exhilarating performances of the work to which over twelve hundred people came from the area. It represented once again the way the Christian language was able to interpret the Millennium experience even for those whose connection with church, either as participants or audience, was minimal. The language still worked and the most moving section was to hear everyone present singing the Millennium version of the Lord's Prayer. It represented the climax of my role as vicar of St Mary's as well, since it symbolised for me the sort of possibilities the Church of England offered as a Christian-language-speaking community in the area, exploring a distinctively Christian description of what was taking place in ordinary people's lives.

Both of these examples indicate to me that there is still an ear and an echo in our society for the Christian language faithfully spoken in lives committed to the service of ordinary people. However, the language has undergone sustained attack during the past two hundred years and speakers will require considerable recovery of confidence in the language if it is going to challenge its detractors. Ordinary Christians are constantly being invited to forget their language. Clergy are also tempted to dilute the force of the language we represent in an attempt to be relevant. Yet paradoxically the pluralist character of our society offers us, once again, the space to embody and articulate distinctive Christian discourse without feeling the necessity to reduce this to a more limited secular speak. Indeed secular speak is itself less secure as a language game than many of its protagonists would hope. Under the challenge of late or post-modernity it is increasingly being seen as a particular and relative dialect rather than a definitive and universally intelligible language.

Talking together

The question which all this raises, therefore, is how ordinary Christian communities in this sort of society are going to recover their language and become confident, fluent speakers of this language. In some way the answer lies in the way languages emerge and are learned. If by language we mean the way we render intelligible the multiple signs which comprise creation and acknowledge that languages are intrinsically social, then languages require communities in order to emerge and develop. Furthermore, if they are to remain part of that linguistic tradition, these communities need to be conscious of how their identity informs the way the language is spoken. Languages are dynamic rather than fixed, they develop in and across time and space and are relational rather than idealistic. Conversation is where languages live, even as texts. Hence the character of the communities who speak a given language will be webbed into the tradition of this language, will be attentive to other speakers as well as having their own distinctive dialects. For example, some might argue that Islam represents a dialect of Christianity, just as Christianity represents a dialect of Judaism. This means that the conversations between the two are not between incommensurable languages but between those who have much in common. This would contrast with the situation between Hinduism and Christianity. Similarly the Enlightenment can be seen as an intensification of the secularising tendencies inherent in certain dialects of Christianity reaching back to the medieval philosophers Duns Scotus and William of Ockham.[3] This pedigree then allows for a meaningful conversation about the character of those intensifications as I noted above.

The implications of this for the church in England must therefore include attention to the character of our Christian language, its local dialects and its capacity to describe the ways of God immanent in the increasingly complex world we are part of. As I will discuss later in this book, this will require awareness that belonging actively to a worshipping Christian community is vital if this confidence and language learning are to happen. Gathering to worship is about undergoing a grammatical check to ensure that we are speaking properly. Without gathering to worship our language slips into an increasingly dislocated slang prey to other vocal influences, which we may not be alert to. Hence the importance of belonging to believe, since the fluency of a speaker is directly related to his or her participation in the community. Worship as language learning is osmotic. As such the worship of different communities will have its own distinctive character relative to the particular community gathered to worship. Dialects will develop in this way. As I found in Wheatley, worship is to enable us to become competent speakers where we are, as ambassadors for the wider community of Christ. We had to learn to speak in a Doncaster dialect of the Christian language. Such competence involves being able to practise the language or make the language work in whatever situations present themselves. One cannot in advance specify how one is going to speak on any given occasion.

What is clear is that this is a social task and a political one. It is social in so far as the resources for language learning do not reside in any one individual. There can be no *'Desert Island Discs'* approach to discipleship. Language presumes a conversational possibility, which is necessarily a social reality rather than a monologue situation. Indeed it will often be among the superficially least articulate of our Christian communities that the language of faith remains purest, since these fragile communities have often had to test this language far more demandingly than those who possess other powers which can be relied upon. Yet it is also a matter of recovering our politics, in the sense that language is correlative to a community, which speaks it and lives it. How that community is ordered for life reflects and informs the way it speaks that language. As such, language is a political gift, since we receive our community's language before we contribute anything distinctive to the way it is spoken. Hence our debt to our community indicates that it is the life of this community which ensures that we can continue to grasp, hear and speak the language. As parents we were only able to recognise Emily's problem with Doncaster English because we were sufficiently English in the widest sense to recognise this dialect as part of our linguistic currency. Similarly I could recognise Street Reach as part of Christian grammar because my awareness, mediated by the church, of the love of Jesus indicated that this was his sort of speech.

Summary

Christian language learning can only properly happen as we are part of an embodied community of fellow speakers who, together, help us to improve our language skills. Such a community needs to be sufficiently widespread to limit the liabilities of our finitude and corruptions. It cannot therefore simply be a local community but must be webbed into the traditions and extensions of its linguistic community. Of course all of us will be relatively fluent in other languages, some of which will be about our nationality, our gender, our history and so on. What the church needs to recover is confidence and fluency in our mother tongue. This, though, will only happen as we recover the pivotal importance of gathering to worship together as the Anglican phrase 'common worship' indicates. For common worship as understood by the English Reformers within the Church of England did not mean that everyone agreed in common about all aspects of worship.[4] Neither did it mean that all forms of worship were to be identical, despite the appearance of the Book of Common Prayer in its various manifestations. Rather it meant that discerning the wisdom of God in life needed the joint participation of laity and clergy in worship. Worship was common in so far as it was a shared exploration, as opposed to a clerically (Rome) or a textually (the Confessions of the Continental Reformers and Puritans) determined discernment. Viewing things from the vantage point of the evangelical tradition, the importance of recovering this understanding of common worship cannot be underestimated as we attempt to speak the Christian language in our day. Only in this way will we be able to reverse the amnesia which besets us and realise the resources of this remarkable language and its correlative community, the church.

3 Marginal worship

'You are what you eat'

Sue, my wife, works in the Special Needs Department of a large comprehensive school in north Doncaster. Its catchment area includes some of the most deprived parts of the borough and many of the youngsters she teaches present complex social problems. However, she is also convinced that one of the more obvious contributors to the behavioural problems she encounters is diet. Many of these young teenagers live on a diet of fast food and drink. Parenting skills, such as how to produce a healthy meal on a regular basis and at a regular time, have been eroded by a combination of work pressures, social breakdown and advertising power. Hence a good number of children presenting special needs, especially in behavioural terms, are also presenting dietary problems.

Diet is a key challenge to Christian communities. While it is certainly the case that phrases such as 'food as fuel', 'garbage in garbage out', 'an army marches on its stomach' and 'you are what you eat' can seem simplistic, there is a truth here which has particular importance for a church seeking to recover confidence in its vocation. Nourishment is fundamental to the life of the Christian community. Unless we pay careful attention to what is nourishing us, then what we will become will not resource us and form us for our vocation as a sign of God's grace in the world. Similarly if our nourishment is inadequate, then our service will be inadequate. Not only will we lack the necessary energy, but our embodied condition will render us unfit for service. A snacking society is a feeble society, surviving but not flourishing.

Worship as nourishment

One of the surprising things I observed during my eight years as vicar of St Mary's in Doncaster was the way the congregation grew. Certainly there was a lot of activity going on as energy was put into visiting, children and young people's work, the occasional offices, social events and the elderly, but the main environment for growth was the Sunday morning service. It was as if what held people in church was discovering what it meant to worship together as a community of considerable diversity. There was nothing particularly spectacular about the morning worship. We did endeavour to make our monthly all-age service as hospitable as we could to the visitors who came with baptism parties. We regarded these services as a sort of shop window for the community to look into the church. Yet even here we remained wedded to a liturgical framework and often sang quite traditional hymns and spirituals. After eight years I was convinced that what was happening was that the community which came on a Sunday was being nourished through word and sacrament and hence an oasis was being created which was attractive to those who either through invitation or initiative came along. This is not to say that everyone who came to a Sunday morning service became an active member of the community. Nor does it mean that we are talking about enormous numbers. The Electoral Roll grew from about 120 to 200 adults during that time, with about 90–110 adults and about 15–25 children being present each Sunday morning towards the end of our time there and about 170 adults and about 35 children attending Sunday worship over the course of a month. However, it was encouraging for all involved to sense that something was growing and for that growth to be happening, nourishment was present.

Worship, belonging and believing

The vital practice of public worship has been lost to the majority of our society and is even a fragile conviction among those disposed to churchgoing.[1] In part this reflects the impact of modern life, as alternatives to church such as shopping, the leisure industry, sport and travel opportunities have challenged the territory of churchgoing. This is often misrepresented as 'secularisation' but, as Grace Davie has pointed out (and certainly my experience of being a vicar would support this), many still claim to believe even if their belonging is very tangential.[2] It is as if they wish the gathered church to act vicariously for them Sunday by Sunday and to be there for the rites of passage, birth, possibly marriage and, even more so, in death. Indeed funerals represent the failure of secularisation to impact upon the majority of society if by secularisation is meant a divorce between a religious description of life and a non-religious one, for funerals represent ontological orientations. While it is true that much exploration of the religious among the population at large is much more anarchic and eclectic, it remains present and, *in extremis,* mainly defaults to Christian symbols rather than to others. In a sense the protagonists of secularism deceive precisely because they claim to represent a tradition and practice which has no community embodiment. It is about not doing things regularly rather than actively representing a way of living which could be subsumed meaningfully under one category. Hence its identity is parasitic upon those who practise their faith, since without this it would be a term with no meaning.

Nevertheless, although there is considerable evidence, as Grace Davie indicates, for believing without belonging in the wider community, and certainly such was the case in Wheatley, this cannot be a satisfactory condition for the baptised since it fails to recognise the formative role of worship. Indeed, in some ways it reflects the pathology of an extreme Protestantism, which locates the church in the individual and renders each person his or her pope. As I mentioned in Chapter 1, this tendency is evident in the weak ecclesiology of much evangelicalism and is not adequately dealt with by regarding the primary purpose of worship as a voluntary acknowledgement of God in a voluntary fellowship of like-minded believers. This ecclesiology simply legitimates the wider cultural dislocation of church and society. Instead, attention needs to be paid to the dynamics of worship which have affinities to the dynamics of eating and drinking. They form bodies and thereby identities. It is no accident that the most holy act of worship is centred round the symbols of a meal.

Without entering into a complex description of the way Jews and Christians have worshipped in the Old and New Testaments, it is apparent that the character of the community at worship was correlative to the character of that worship. The prophets, in particular, addressed in the first instance not the wider society, but the people of God, and indicated that the integration of liturgical and political worship was essential if they were to represent the light of God to the world. In addition, Jesus' own ministry, particularly his cleansing of the temple, was a direct challenge to those who dissolved the bonds between love of God and love of neighbour that he, as Messiah, sought to maintain. Worship and politics are symbiotic. Both need to be truthful if they are not to corrupt each other, and belonging forms believing in a way unavailable to those who do not belong.

Going public

Holiness or sanctification, the setting apart of a people as a witness or sign of the divine activity of God in the created order, emerges out of truthful worship. It is here that the dynamic intercourse between God and the community transforms ordinary people into more faithful 'God-bearers'. Gathering for public worship, though not the exclusive context for this encounter, is certainly its primary location. For English Reformers, such as Richard Hooker, this was why public prayer is more important than private prayer. Public prayer as common prayer involves the embodied community, laity and clergy, exploring the grace of God in their discipleship.[3] It challenges the community with what it actually means to practise faith rather than allowing individual fantasies to replace the complexities of a living community. It asks of a given community how its life can be offered to God and received back from him, infused with his grace. It forces an individualistically orientated culture to explore what 'Our Father in heaven' as opposed to 'My Father in heaven' implies for discipleship in life. Over time it forms a community into a people whose exposition of the holiness of God is related to the particulars of their environment as it webs or contextualises the variety of stories present in the gathered and wider communities. In this way it forms people to see themselves and their context more clearly in terms of explicit Christian description and limits the corrosive effects of alien languages upon this primary tongue.

A healthy outlook

Gathering to worship publicly, therefore, becomes a primary calling for Christians, particularly in an age when communal bonds
have been subject to many acidic pressures, not the least of which
is the narcissistic character of consumerism. Worship is primarily
outward looking despite popular suggestions that it represents
attention to the 'inner world'. Christian worship properly liber-
ates Christians from self-preoccupation as it directs their
attention away from themselves towards God. Certainly the character of divine transcendence in Christian theology is more
complex than spatial metaphors suggest. The 'otherness' of God
is precisely evident in God's capacity to be intimate with us by
the Spirit, yet distinctively different from us as Father. Similarly
Christian worship indicates that the church never enters 'territory' uninhabited by the reigning Christ. How else would St Paul
as a Jew and from a sea-phobic tradition have engaged in so
many maritime journeys if he was not convinced that the
ascended Christ was already ahead of him as well as with him?[4]

Nevertheless it is this attention to the other which will form the
Christian community into one able to welcome the stranger as
Jesus did and represent a community secure in the knowledge
that the future is not in its control. Such attention will offer the
community opportunity and time to explore what it means to
serve local people without having to do everything or to get
everything right. Such attention will represent the most important political statement which needs to be made, namely that God
in Jesus Christ reigns and that that reign guarantees the contingency of all other claims to rule in life. Such attention will form
particular gathered communities of worship to see what the distinctive agenda of God for their calling is, an agenda which will
not be identical to that of any other church even if it is part of the
wider sign of God's mission in life. It will thereby free churches
from the corrosive competitive tendencies which come with com-
parisons, without implying that there is nothing to learn from
analogous service by other Christian communities.

To give an example, when I was assistant priest of a small
Anglican church in what was then categorised as a 'white' area
in Grahamstown, South Africa, St Paul's College arranged a

placement which included black students of Xhosa pedigree. As part of the exploration of worship and formation these students taught the congregation how to sing parts of the liturgy in Xhosa. Whilst the rendition was somewhat elementary, it began to transform that small community in a number of striking ways. First it established respect for Xhosa and by implication Xhosa culture. In so doing it began in a very limited way to undo years of apartheid corruption. Second, it changed the power dynamics in the congregation as those whom apartheid categorised as second class became the teachers of those whom apartheid believed to possess the resources of civilisation and power. Third, it symbolised that this congregation was part of the African church rather than remaining an outpost of the Church of England. Fourth, it enabled friendships to emerge across the social divides of that society.

These were very limited effects and, to many activists, somewhat tokenist and relatively impotent. However, as sign and as beginning, they contributed to the deconstruction of apartheid and to the building up of what Archbishop Tutu called the 'Rainbow People of God'. Right worship formed clearer sight, which led to transformed lives. Certainly this was a slow process and it could be said that the previous worship of this church, like many others in white areas, had failed to reflect a truthful worship. Yet, in some sense, the very dynamic and contextual character of worship is represented in this case history, since it took the participation of Christians who represented the stranger to this white community at this particular time, to enable a more truthfully worshipping community to emerge. This is a reminder that all worship is an unfinished and contingent experience. To coin a Reformation slogan, it is a reminder that the church must live *semper reformanda*, always needing reform.

Not simply pew fodder

If, as I have argued, public worship is where the dynamic interplay of God with us is given its most attentive focus, then the participants in this interplay take on particular significance. Much has been written and preached about the character of God as the primary agent in this transforming relationship. Less attention has been given to the contribution of the worshippers, particularly in contextual terms. Formally their place has been recognised, but this tends to understate the creative contribution their participation makes to the ongoing expression of the things of God. As mentioned in the previous chapter, Christian discipleship is like learning a language with which to make best sense of life's journey. While grasping this language is not confined to the embodied church, given the Spirit's grace in all creation, the embodied church is certainly an intensive language-learning environment with public worship as the particular focus of this. It is as if here Christian language is inculcated and its grammar indicated. Yet in this language lab, dialects also develop which are reflections of the way worship has happened and is happening among this group of gathered Christians in a way that cannot simply be typed and transported to other contexts. In a significant way this is because the participants are always in some place and in some time, rather than abstract and independent of time. The implications for ordinary worshippers are apparent. Every worshipper's story and contribution is gathered up in the offering of worship and informs the way the Christian language is spoken in this particular place. Instead of cloning, worship is actually about celebrating the harmony of difference, being part of a choir or orchestra conducted by Christ. Once again the insights about common worship become evident. For common worship is primarily about enabling the whole church in all its diversity to explore what it means to worship God today as a community with a history that is carried in its memory.

This is a hard perspective to convey in the sort of society England has become in the light of the post-Enlightenment tradition. Here the twin pressures of conformity to ideals and quantifiable success make it difficult for church communities to explore the distinctiveness of their callings, as opposed to looking for the sort of ideals and successes which concur with the spirit of the age, and seeking to emulate these in detail. During my time in Doncaster I have seen a number of clergy resign or retire on the grounds of ill health. While each story has its own peculiarities, it struck me time and again that underlying each was a tension between expectations and reality. It was as if the church they had in their minds, developed in a different context and with a different community or idealised from participation in para-church groups, did not materialise. Burnout followed, burnout which was more about the loss of vision and confidence in the grace of God active in that community than about over-energetic ministry. To my mind they were oppressed by the ideals of church they sought to import and thereby impose, much akin to the frustration of English colonials with Africans who couldn't be formed into black English people.

The character of worship I believe is to call into question this approach and to restore the primary exploration and formation to the local community. Whatever comes from elsewhere, either in the consciousness of the clergy or in the exposure of the church to the broader Christian community, needs to be seen as a secondary commentary on the local reading. Recovering the significance of ordinary churchgoers, it seems to me, is one of the keys to the restoration of the confidence of the Christian community at large. As those who occupy our pews become agents in worship, so the church will reflect its incarnational vocation to be a contextual sign of the grace of God. The universal love of God can only be known through the myriad of particular expressions.

It is as the love of God is seen to engage so many different people in dialects which they can understand and contribute to, that the Gospel will be seen to be of universal currency. Indeed this is where the international and trans-historical church itself becomes important. It indicates and displays the way other pilgrims have been and are being formed in the grace of God. In so doing the differences actually serve the whole, since they indicate the character of the whole as the rainbow people of God, as Archbishop Tutu asserted. They also check local excesses, since differences challenge local practices to give an account of their own traditions in a way that can be recognised by other Christian communities as part of the same story of God. One of the tragedies of South Africa was when the Dutch Reformed Church of the apartheid era believed that within its own locale lay all the resources for a truthful worship of God in a segregated manner. The rest of the Reformed Church disagreed with this as did the vast majority of other Christian traditions. As a result of their unwillingness to listen to their fellow Christians' critiques, South Africa became a racist state and the church was divided and tarnished by the legacy of this introspection.

Summary

Worship should be about the offering of life by a particular community attentive to its context, yet in conversation with the wider Christian community. Such worship will form a particular community into holiness appropriate for its contextual vocation. It will give wisdom and sight to that community, enabling it to discern the particular forms of service appropriate to the time and place. These forms of service will seek to be relevant to the vocation God's grace mediates in and through the practice of worshipping together. They will not, therefore, be in thrall to whatever are the superficial demands of a given context, since the intention is to work from the agenda of the Spirit of God rather than from concerns unformed by the practice of worship. Of course, given the character of God revealed in the history of Israel, the Jews, the history of the church and expressed, iconically, in Jesus Christ, this will be about compassionate service of those estranged from God and ourselves. Hence to give priority to the Spirit of God discerned through worship is not to imply an arbitrary and capricious service.

What public worship will also entail is a noticeable difference between those who worship thus and those who do not. Without implying that this is a salvific difference, it is certainly a character difference, since, as indicated above, worship is not simply response as duty or choice, but is about transformation. To be involved in the active worship of God cannot but be transforming, since God is the guarantor of the process. Sometimes to us that transformation may seem lacking or inadequate. However, we are not the judge of that. Indeed sometimes the very people we least like become God's angels to test our trust that, if God's grace can meet me, then there is no reason why that grace cannot be attending to this most objectionable person. This is a further reason why belonging matters. We might otherwise miss the opportunity to be visited by angels.

4 Marginal mission

Body beautiful

In the previous chapter we noted that worship, particularly public worship, transforms, webs people together, illuminates the particular journey ahead for the community, indicates to that community its tasks, and in all of this improves the language skills of that body. In so doing it nourishes a community, thereby forming it into one which acts as a sign of the grace of God in the midst of its setting. Such communities find themselves inevitably centrifugal as the character of the missionary God infuses their own identity. Similarly as they are sanctified they are in a sense divinised, that is, they begin to see the divine agenda and are thereby able to discern what is relevant service at this time and in this context. In all of this God is the primary agent, with the community as an active listener. There is both challenge and relief here since all is not dependent upon human agency alone.

In my present role as Director of Ministry, I find myself travelling around South Yorkshire and parts of the East and West Riding taking services and visiting clergy. As mentioned in Chapter 1, I am constantly amazed by the tenacity of fragile churches acting as witnesses to the grace of God in their areas. All represent very ordinary people who are committed to the worship and service of God. Each active member regards him- or herself as an agent of the Gospel, whose presence really matters to the survival and flourishing of that community. Each person matters and it matters to welcome others in even if the spiritual landscape seems more akin to a desert than an oasis. Worship is usually passionate and profound. Certainly many are elderly people, some are disabled mentally or physically, but in a youth 'body-beautiful' obsessed culture, they act as a sign of the grace of God. Unless church is as they are, then what gathers is indicative not of God's universal call but of God's call only to the able. These fragile communities are the barometer of the health of the wider church. If they disappear because the wider church does not support them, then the Christian sign will be diminished. A missionary symbol will have been lost both to the active church-goers in these areas and to the communities they are set among.

Embodied apologetics is a shorthand way of describing this primary dimension of the church's mission.[1] As has often been stressed, the church's mission is to follow the mission of God, which is wider than the church and is the way God is bringing in his kingdom. Following that mission in the first instance means allowing God to make a community more distinctively his, through the practices of worship. In short it means being made into a visible sign. It is as this happens that the glory of God is most explicit: ordinary people's lives offered to God in worship are offered back infused with the light and love of God. Of course, like the glory of the cross, this is not a glory always recognised by its bearers or by those who meet them. Nevertheless the participation with and commitment of God to a people who call on his name is intrinsic to his character. The scriptural narrative, as Ronald Thiemann points out, is in some sense verified as promises are seen to be fulfilled and, as Karl Barth points out, the character of God revealed in the Scriptures is that God is always experienced as 'God-with-us'.[2] Hence we cannot avoid absorbing the fragrance of God as we 'draw near'. Equally, as we worship we enter not only the language lab of the faith but also the training arena. Worship trains us to become a people whose way of life embodies the story of God-with-us. As we practise our faith, so we become more ascetic, that is more athletic in our display of this graceful transforming reality.[3] As we practise our faith by working co-operatively with God in his mission we come to see more clearly what work we are to do. The fact that we label the prayers of the Church of England 'offices' is simply a reminder that our identity implies this sort of work as the priesthood of Christ. Our mission, in part, is to be a community regularly offering the world to God for his redemption.

Mission on margins

Training is about becoming more able to engage in the mission implied by our identity as Christ's church. As we noted above, this necessitates discovering the reign of God as Jesus did, among the edge situations of life. In God's kingdom the periphery is the centre and the liminal is the core. This is why it strikes me as odd that the general assumption of the successful church is that it is the one where the most people are and where the finances are most secure and where the staff are most remarkably gifted. A cursory reading of the gospels should indicate that the most successful exemplar of God's reign was the most liminal of all figures, even dying outside the symbolic centre of Judaism, Jerusalem.

When we knew we were to return to England from South Africa a year or so earlier than expected, the question of where we should go became somewhat acute. South Africa had been a turbulent experience from which we had learned a great deal and involved in this learning was the challenge to work on the margins. Now margins or border areas vary from person to person, so our margins might seem relatively tame to some folk, but when the Bishop of Sheffield offered us the opportunity to go to inner urban Doncaster, this seemed to be the next liminal location for us. It represented the challenge of living and serving communities totally different from my background, even though my wife's heritage included analogous sorts of communities in the Diocese of Carlisle. To work in an inner urban parish of very mixed constituency in one of the lowest churchgoing areas of the country seemed to be the very sort of training ground we needed to grow. It would test us to the limit and require that we approach the situation in much the same attitude as when going to live in a foreign country. We would need to listen to the locals, learn to see what we were looking at and try to become proficient in the local Christian dialect. After eight years we were still being trained.

Mission is about margins. It is about looking over the edge of our securities and taking risks with God who is before us as well as with us. Mission depends upon worship and prayer in order that we may learn to see what is in front of our eyes. I remember once standing in a field with a farmer and saying that he and I were not looking at the same cattle. Physiologically the animals were registering in our consciousness as cattle, but his farming pedigree meant that what he saw there was quite different from my superficial grasp of the situation. I was once told a story of a young man who went to central Africa for a short period. During that time he employed a local man to work in his garden. However, the work of this employee did not appear to the expatriate to be of a high enough standard. As a result he decided to discipline the man and began to remonstrate with him about his work. The consequence was that the man smiled, which antagonised his employer. The more the latter chided his employee the more the employee smiled until, exasperated, he sacked him. It was only later, when recounting this story to a friend who had been in the country for a longer period of time, that he learned the local custom that when a superior is chastising an inferior, the latter smiles in acknowledgement of the offence. To his horror he realised that he had failed to see what was going on before his eyes.

Mission becomes mis-focused when we assume that without worshipping and training with the community of faith we can strike out and serve God. We have to be trained to see what the mission is not only in its general character but in its particular focus. The contextual character of church implies that there is a distinctive mission challenge for each community of faith, just as the New Testament represents a very pluralist notion of mission in the gospels and letters. The Colossians are not expected to represent the mission of Christ in identical terms to the Corinthians. Matthew's church has a vocation distinct from the Johannine communities. Yet it is these very ambiguous communities which are the vehicles for mission. The Corinthians are a problematic lot, yet God's call is for them to get on with being church where they are. Similarly the Roman church has its particular calling to represent the Gentile mission in a way that has affinities with the theology of Ephesians but is certainly not identical.

Dealing with the realities where we are located and amidst the people of God gathered in that place and time is a vital aspect of Christian mission. Our scriptural story indicates that to do anything significant within this sort of world even God had to respect time and place. Indeed one of the dangers of talking loosely about incarnation is that it becomes a sort of abstract idea rather than a way of forcing us to attend to the specificities of where we are and of the people among whom we find ourselves. It can be very attractive, philosophically and theologically, to imagine the character of God incarnate. However, the challenges of incarnate mission can be very demanding and costly as most clergy will testify. Yet it is precisely in the recovery of the messy untidy qualities of embodied mission that the Christian story is best seen in action and, for Anglicans, this is what is represented in the notion of parish church. As Archbishop Rowan Williams reminded the licensed ministers of the Diocese of Sheffield in his Shrove Tuesday addresses of 2002, the Greek word *paroikos* means 'migrant', while the Greek word *ecclesia* means 'the citizens' assembly'. The vocation of church is to enable those wandering around in a given area, who are presently marginal to the ecclesia, to have the opportunity to become part of the assembly of God. Parish mission and ministry is therefore about offering that opportunity to a territory of spiritual vagrants. Historically, in England, this has indeed been delineated by parish boundaries. However, with the legacy of urbanisation, and social and intellectual mobility, the notion of parish may need to become more flexible as measurements of identity other than simply geography will need to be looked at. Indeed this is already happening in new forms of church which are being explored.[4]

What is exciting but also stressful about mission on the margins, or borders, is that here is where the risk of life is felt most keenly and where instabilities and vulnerabilities offer opportunity to be creative. I remember visiting Uganda as an adult after having left over 28 years ago and being driven to the border area in the west. Not only was there a rebel raid on a town that we had visited the day before with many killed and injured, but we saw displaced people surviving in conditions of considerable discomfort. Yet people were improvising and finding new ways to live now that the old ways were no longer available to them. Equally they were focused upon what they could achieve in the immediate present, since their future was insecure. They had little to defend from the past and they could not afford to dream too wildly about the future. Getting on with what was in hand became a top priority.

Mission in England is now mission from and on the margins. Certainly for those of us associated with the Church of England, resting in the 'security' of being central to the social order is no longer an option. Indeed, while we can debate the extent to which what has been called 'The Constantinian Settlement' is still viable, it is certainly not as it was. England is far less a society of English Christians exploring its liturgical worship in church and its political worship through its lay parliament, even taking account of the recent 2001 census.[5] Elements of this remain and such a view of society, as I have hinted at above, is by no means dead and buried. However, dissent from this arrangement has become the rhetorical norm, together with an assault upon what are its perceived privileges. While active churchgoing for public worship has probably never been a majority experience, even in the days of the Acts of Uniformity, it is certainly the case now that regular attenders at public worship are a small fraction of the population. The growth we saw in attendance at public worship in Doncaster has nevertheless to be set against the parish population figures of nearly six thousand. Over an eight-year period, including all the occasional offices, Sunday services, children and youth provision and interaction with community groups, the number of people who came to a church service was certainly more than the parish population. However, it would be naïve to imagine that such tentative belonging represented a recognition among most of these folk of the centrality of the worshipping community or even the centrality of belonging in some way to the church as a public body. Like a public convenience, the church was a utility for certain times of life, but not a community into which people felt consciously grafted. For the committed, liminality and marginality are the norm.

Mission as sign language

Nevertheless, as my analogy from the borders of Uganda implies, this offers the gathered community creative challenge. No longer called upon by wider society to represent a total politics for society as a whole, the gathered community, either in national and diocesan or in parish terms, can now explore fresh ways of witness. Nationally this may mean renegotiating what 'Establishment' means so as to develop the underlying notion from the Elizabethan Settlement, which was that as many as were able to share together in the broadly Christian pedigree which has formed England, should become part of that establishment. Other religious traditions, which have been less formative of the identity and values of the country, would nevertheless be seen as active conversation partners. They would ensure that the myth of the 'naked square' often articulated by secularists does not represent itself as an innocent neutral space while actually masking undeclared agendas of interest groups which have no identifiable or accountable tradition. Their importance would be in ensuring that society did not become introspectively anthropocentric and hence totalitarian.

An exploration of the contemporary meaning of Establishment would also involve revisiting the counselling role of church leaders in the sort of society we now represent. Historically, as spiritual counsellors of the monarch, bishops had a contributory role in the political arrangements of England, which is now embodied in their place in the House of Lords. As this polity has become more concerned with democratic accountability, the question of whether the bishops' counselling role has become too closely associated with the explicit exercise of unaccountable power has raised questions about their role and its legitimacy. More valuable may be an exploration into other ways of representing spiritual counsel to the sovereign in parliament, which are no longer associated with executive power. Such counsel, in the present ecumenically open era, should include leaders of other communities within the Christian tradition and also other significant non-Christian faith traditions present in the country.

Mission in more local contexts needs to be correlative to the way distinctive Christian communities 'see' the challenges before them and are able to discern appropriate sign language that would engage them. Speaking as a priest serving in the Church of England, I would argue that diocese and parish (or equivalent) each have their own discernment to do. The diocese is the local church in Anglican thinking; that is, the unit of church whose locale is embodied in the person of the bishop and to whom all Anglicans are accountable in that diocese. In the mission of this church dioceses will need to explore what it means to share the Gospel in a way attentive to life as it is and as it has emerged in this area, by engaging in conversations within and beyond its constituency. Again this will often be about becoming aware of the border areas not only between itself and others but also within itself. However, it will also involve greater attention to the polity of the diocese, or the society of the diocese, which, for historic reasons, has been neglected. Dioceses will need to become more coherent realities in order that the mission of the church is not simply a series of eccentric responses without any accountability to the whole. Similarly, for creative mission to happen, there will need to be much greater inter-parish work than has traditionally been the case, mediated through the bishop's oversight. This will not only release and share resources, and encourage mutual learning of what the Gospel might mean in different areas of a diocese, but will also enable sector and specialist ministry to contribute to particular contexts and thereby strengthen the sense of being a community of friends travelling together.

At a parish level, mission will be responsive to more particular interpretations of God's calling with an emphasis upon diversity, a multitude of distinct, yet related, signs. However, the liminal character of many parish churches means that the gathered community will need to become more distinctive communities than has been the case in the past if their mission is to have impact. They will need to see themselves as quasi-religious orders, with a calling to signify the Gospel in that place. This may be helped by congregations adopting rules of life, or mission statements, which focus the calling of that community for that time and place. It may need to involve internal structural changes to enable greater congregational activism. This is what Steven Croft has emphasised in his call for 'Transforming Christian Communities' which, though having affinities to housegroups and cell groups, are characterised by a particular mission focus. Parish mission will represent a commitment to be present as a community of public worship open to the wider community. It will represent an active community of hospitable friends whose way of life is about welcoming others into the conscious hospitable friendship of God. Hence it will certainly mean imagining creative ways of being church and of engaging with others in the area and also listening and conversing with folk beyond the gathered church.

In our own diocese, two creative ways of exploring this are being pioneered. First, like a number of other dioceses, we are exploring new ways of being church alongside existing parish and sector models. This includes planting churches, looking at forms of ministry which are explicitly mission minded, and also developing our educational responsibilities. In addition we have been involved in a project called 'Discerning Church Vocation'.[6] Under this initiative each parish has been asked to invite representatives from the area to begin a conversation about how the church could serve and engage with the challenges of that area at a series of public meetings characterised by hospitality. It is not about delegating to others the agenda of the Gospel. Rather it is listening to hear the voice of Christ already engaged in mission in the area through the stories of those invited to share their insights and wisdom. In some of our inner urban areas, this has led to a partnership with other local groups and indeed the state, which, though carrying risks, is actually a symbolic rejection of the superficial secularism which used to characterise government agencies and indeed church authorities in the middle of the last century.[7] In this, though, is further recognition that the voice of Christ is best heard when we are liminal. Liminal people are not powerless people. Rather they are de-centred people who see things differently and in a way not confused by pretensions to controlling their destiny. As a result this offers them the possibility of critical insight, since their perspective is not driven by the will to power. Liminal churches can therefore listen to their wider communities with ears and eyes critically aware of the voice of God present in what is being said or unsaid.

Mission as patient presence

For Christians following the mission of God, therefore, there needs first to be a certain tactical introspection before a second more outward-focused engagement.[8] This tactical introspection is about becoming more aware of what a Christian community is as a society of friends, aware of the gracious hospitality and presence of God-with-us and travelling together as a pilgrim people inviting others to join us on this journey. It is about being aware of having our own stories of life integrated within a much richer and fuller epic, the Story of God. It is about offering to others the opportunity to have their own stories located in a way far more substantial and significant than the limited narratives that have emerged in late modernity. It is about talking up the significance of ordinary people's lives as part of a cosmic and indeed eternal drama. Hence such introspection is about recovering confidence that following the mission of God wherever we are is about sharing in the most wonderful story that can be told. It is indeed Good News.

Nevertheless this introspection will also force us to confront our past as a community whose history is ambiguous and from whom many have dissented for good reason. This is especially true of the Church of England. A proper humility about what this term means to many in our society needs to be apparent. Mission requires that we understand why in general and particular ways the Christian story has lost the confidence of our society, even if, we may wish to argue, that society is itself partly culpable here in its capitulation to superficiality and instant gratification. This is particularly evident in our northern urban areas where memories of boss-driven church attendance remain fixed in the minds of descendants of employees, and hierarchical practices, such as the one mentioned in Chapter 1, remain deep wounds in the collective memory. Mission cannot proceed without addressing the legacy of this ambiguous past.

Furthermore such introspection will indicate that the calling of the church, in its various expressions, is to achieve today a more evident political identity than has been the case in the immediate past. The old English Settlement imagined by Richard Hooker is no longer viable, if ever it was. Perhaps the image now is not of one settlement attempting to include all in an encompassing way, but a settlement which indicates the broad tradition within which contemporary English society is set and which is illustrated in the varieties of Christian communities which gather to worship regularly and which seek to order their communal life in a more political way. English society would then be faithful to its identity, while the gathering of committed worshippers would offer illustration of the life-giving possibilities which embodying this politics more substantially would open up. In this way going to church might become engaging. As mentioned above, this, I believe, was partly why St Mary's in Doncaster grew. It became a community people wanted to be part of because life flourished here in a rich way. Certainly it was costly. The community had to raise their giving to sustain the mission and fabric of the church and the income did grow from about £21,000 p.a. to about £45,000 p.a. over the eight years, with over £75,000 given for a building project at the same time. Simply becoming aware of what the possibilities of being part of a Christian community might mean released all sorts of energies and creativities which were latent in people.

In addition, what enabled mission to happen was the church's loitering with intent. Being around is one of the basic premises for mission. In an age suspicious of the stranger, church can easily become estranged and strange. Inviting school children to visit church in Doncaster was an indication of this estrangement. Many had never consciously been in this or any other church building before and it was fascinating to watch the awe on their faces as the glory of the building and its story dawned upon them. There were sermons in stone. Yet it took me two years of patient waiting to be allowed access into the local county primary schools, perhaps because of the ambivalent memory of church in these communities. Similarly, as parish priest, walking to school with my children and dogs not only offered informal pastoral contact with people. It also enabled me to become part of the scenery to the extent that when I completed my calling in that parish it was hard for me to walk or cycle through the parish without being engaged in conversation by someone. Loitering with intent as a recognisable community and, in the case of church leaders, as the public representative of that community is an underrated mission practice. Like most valuable things, it is non-quantifiable, but when it does not happen its absence is corrosive of other mission activities of the church.

Mission is often conceived of as akin to the revivalist meetings of the nineteenth century, which mutated into Billy Graham rallies in the twentieth. These should not be ridiculed, since they brought to life many people who otherwise would not have been reached. However, they depended upon a general consciousness of the Christian faith, often inculcated in Sunday school, which is increasingly absent from many of our communities. Hence a more valuable strategy is for the local church to become a hospitable and serving community in a given context so that people may once again be fascinated by what the Gospel represents. Indeed with the demise of the sort of Sunday school experience, which offered an effective inoculation against Christianity among past generations, there is anecdotal evidence, such as my own, that churches are now regarded as mysteries rather than mind-manipulators. As noted above, the response of school children and young people to church buildings is noticeably different to what it was even thirty years ago. There is ignorance but not hostility and creative hospitality provides nourishment for positive memories to be embedded in a way contrary to many older people's recollections of their youth.

The way Alpha has helped churches to explore this hospitable mission should also not be diminished. While there is an element of the 'fast food culture' about Alpha, it has enabled ordinary churches to rediscover one of their core identities: hospitable communities sharing word and sacrament. Similarly there is also evidence that churches are being seen as significant communities in many of our more deprived regions since they and their ministers are still around after everyone else has fled. In my own visitations of clergy in the Diocese of Sheffield I have noticed that the more fragile churches are often most engaged in the traditional parish ministry of active mission to the surrounding community, through schools, regeneration initiatives, use of church premises, evangelistic work with youngsters and so on.

Summary

Mission is often about ecclesial bodies patiently loitering with intent in a given area. Mission is about following and living in God's time and hence we can take time to wait and see when and where we are to be engaged. Mission involves having worshipful eyes, which are trained to see and act on God's agenda. Mission involves representing an embodied sign of the grace of God in various contexts. Mission involves sharing the Gospel where we are and among those with whom we share life. It is about a Christian community in conversation with God and with its neighbourhood.

5 Marginal story

Making music

Reading a musical score, even for someone who is musically literate, cannot compare with hearing a piece of music played. Yet the score matters since it conveys the record or memory of what was in the composer's imagination. However, to play the music is to bring the score to life and to play the music inevitably involves an interpretation, which distances the music from the imagination of its composer. If the composer is still alive it may be possible to ask to what extent this rendition reflects her or his hopes. Otherwise the composer is unable to determine how the music will be played. The score offers formal parameters but not ones which imply precision. What informs the experience of the music is the character, capabilities and sensitivities of those playing it at the time. Without them the music remains a dormant possibility. With them it becomes embodied as sound.[1]

Scripture as score

The analogy from above, though perhaps somewhat crude, is a helpful one when it comes to grasping the relationship between Scripture and church. Scripture is a score, which the church seeks to perform. Scripture is indicative of the way we should play the music of God or sing God's song. However, the actual singing and how that singing is interpreted is relative to the community which is singing or playing. In addition we need to stretch the analogy further since the presence of the Spirit in life implies that the score for God's song or music is not confined to the Scriptures alone. These represent the classic expression of the way the people of God are to sing or play God's music. However, this playing is itself an interpretation relative to time and place. It is indicative in the sense that it trains us to become skilled singers. What it does not do is determine the exact way the song will be sung in ever new situations. This is the role of the Spirit who, while in the church, is not confined to the church.[2]

Inevitably this dynamic singing or playing means that not all singers and players will feel comfortable with the way the music is being sung or played at any one time. I recall the ambivalence with which classical musicians regarded the Electric Light Orchestra in the 1970s as it tried to jazz up classical music. Equally there will be contention about the character of the score beyond the Scriptures and over who should discern this score. As I noted above, this contention can be seen in the different ways God's life is discerned by different Christian communities. Roman Catholics hold that this church discernment is located in the magisterium and especially in the papacy. The Reformed Churches tried to distil the boundaries of the Spirit's leading in their Confessions. Anglicans have sought to locate it in the dynamic relationship between Scripture, tradition and sound learning mediated through common worship (that is clergy and laity together) and various types of synod. Pentecostals have located it in the discernment of the local gathering of the Spirit-filled Christian congregation.

In the era between the resurrection and the second advent of Christ, such contentions are inevitable and remind Christians that at present we see in a glass darkly. However, from what I have argued above, it seems clear to me that the quality of our attention to God in worship and learning will inform our capacities to discern the score of the Spirit in life. Furthermore this will enable us to grasp Scripture better. Scripture is Scripture after all, because there is a community in existence which looks at these texts as foundational for its life and identity.

This is what excited me and challenged me as a priest when I grappled with what it meant to listen to Scripture as part of the church in South Africa and as part of the church in England. At one level both represented belonging to the church of God, yet the contexts were so different that transposing insights from one context to the other could not be done simplistically. Ironically I was more alert to the contextual issues of South Africa than I was to those of Doncaster and the north of England, since I had studied the former's history more carefully and was more aware of the particularities of that part of the world. Like many English clergy, my training had not asked me to undertake the same level of study and attention to the particularities of English identities. The undeclared assumption was that a common-sense view of things was adequate. As I served in Doncaster I became aware that reading Scripture in this environment asked of me a more profound attention to the pedigree of the town and its environment of South Yorkshire. I became aware that the relationship between the town and its satellite mining townships also informed how and why the scriptural narrative was responded to in the ambivalent way it was. I became aware that the particular history of the Church of England in this area informed the unwillingness of many folk to risk worshipping and being formed in this tradition and thereby becoming part of a community rhetorically seeking to listen to God in this way. This was not because they were intrinsically hostile to God, but because their memory of what church, especially what the Church of England represented, rendered them unwilling to participate in practices which the church believed would enable them to become competent readers of Scripture. Past musicians had left too discordant a memory and present players often represented too different a musical style.

What was interesting, however, was that the score was played regularly at certain key moments of life (baptisms, marriages, funerals and remembrance services) when cohorts of folk would engage with the score of Scripture. It was a long and slow piecemeal mission to graft people from such backgrounds into the practising community. Indeed doing so involved St Mary's seeking to become a hospitable community able to sacrifice its own preferred ways of playing the music in order to enable those from different backgrounds to participate. Interestingly this sacrifice often meant accepting what to some churchgoers represented an uncomfortable approach to playing the score of Scripture in services of worship. Yet in seeking to become such a hospitable community St Mary's found itself surprised by the arrival of folk from the surrounding streets who had not been associated with the church for many years. In one case during my fifth year as vicar and as a result of funeral ministry, two women came to church. They then brought three more friends. Later three of the five were confirmed, all of whom are now regulars. Scripture can only be heard when the gathered community faithfully worships, is formed into a competent scripture readership, is alert to its context and thereby embodies something of what Scripture is about. Unless this happens, the score of Scripture remains simply marks on paper.

The insufficiency of Scripture[3]

There is therefore a sense in which even the most conservative evangelical in his or her engagement with the Bible reflects the insufficiency of Scripture. The Scriptures require competent readers if they are to generate their music and such readers are necessarily part of a tradition and society of readers who both equip and critique each other's readings. Reading the Scriptures will force us to read them with others, particularly those who find our readings perplexing.

An example of this is the debate over homosexuality. As part of an attempt to reflect upon my childhood I returned to Uganda for a visit organised by the Church Mission Society just after the Lambeth Conference of 1998 which had involved a sharp division within the Anglican Communion over how homosexuality should be interpreted in the light of Scripture. I was particularly interested in listening to how Christians within this Communion, but from a different vantage point (i.e., non-western), were grappling with this sort of interpretative challenge. Having worked in South Africa, I was aware that the way the issue was being looked at there was in the categories of liberation and justice. Almost alone of the sub-Saharan Anglicans, the Church of the Province of Southern Africa was asserting that the question of homosexuality could not simply be answered in the traditional way. However, I suspected that this was also because the Anglican Church in Southern Africa was more 'western' in its orientation than the rest of the continent and could not be seen as representative of a non-western reading of Scripture. Much of the anti-apartheid theology articulated in South Africa was parasitic upon the legacy of liberation theology and its pedigree in the western theological tradition.[4]

To my dismay, the response to the Lambeth debate which I heard in Uganda represented a most inadequate engagement with Scripture. The group I was with were attending a service at

Makerere University Chapel in Kampala when the University Chaplain used the occasion to preach a 'biblical sermon' on homosexuality. This sermon not once referred to any scriptural texts nor did it engage with any hermeneutical and contextual issues surrounding these texts and their interpretation. Its understanding of the Lambeth debate consisted of quotations from a leading article of *The Times* newspaper and the preacher exploited the occasion to lambaste the western churches as corrupt. In short, it was an opportunity to represent the African church as the faithful bearer of the faith and to reverse the legacy of British imperialism. Ironically it represented modernist 'western' fundamentalism at its worst, revealing thereby the legacy of British imperialism.

At the time I was too disorientated to be able to engage with the speaker. We had only been in the country for twenty-four hours and my sense of identity was being disturbed by floods of childhood memories evoked by everything I saw, memories which were rapidly causing me to feel depressed as the legacy of twenty-five years of political and economic turmoil, war, AIDS and debt were evident everywhere. I remember thinking that the place looked almost identical to my childhood thirty years earlier, but as if no one had painted anything or fixed the potholes. Nevertheless, later the group raised our concerns with some of the younger Ugandan Christians who were with us. Our conversation disclosed that the history of the church in Uganda, established in the martyrdom of page boys who would not tolerate the monarch's homosexual practices, combined with the traditions of promiscuity which were driving AIDS, meant that questions of sexual practice, marriage and the family were highly sensitive in Uganda at that time. Nevertheless, there was also a feeling that the issue was being sidelined rather than addressed. The scriptural debate was therefore masking a predetermined conclusion. The issue was being represented as a western pathology which did not exist in African society and should be resisted without serious attention to the concerns it raised. Arguably a contextual but inadequate engagement with the story of Scripture was taking place.

What this discloses is that there can be no 'innocent' or 'objective' readings of the Scriptures. Certainly the majority of

Christians to date have regarded the matter of homosexual practice in terms of clear prohibition. Texts which are presumed to
refer to same-sex relationships are always antagonistic to them, it
is claimed, and therefore Christians should be so today.[5] However, other Christians, predominantly raised by those in churches
influenced by the legacy of post-Enlightenment criticism and
modern medical science, have questioned whether the texts are
speaking of the contemporary phenomenon called 'homosexuality'. This, they argue, is a condition which was diagnosed in the
nineteenth century and reflects an involuntary sexual identity orientated to the same sex. The scriptural texts, when seen in their
context, refer to people presumed to be contradicting their sexual
identities at a time when such identities were believed to be correlative to biological identity. Hence, just as women were
assumed be the 'weaker sex' in all areas of public life because
they were anatomically less powerful than men, so sexual identity was assumed to be unequivocally indicated by genitalia.
Most western Christians would not accept that women's capacities in public life are intrinsically limited by such presumptions
about their anatomy despite evidence in the Bible of subordina-
tionism, so the question of sexual identity cannot be presumed to
be determined by superficial readings of ancient texts. Whatever
revelation means in Christian thinking within the Anglican tradition, it does not mean an attempt to 'freeze-frame' ancient society
and its contextual grasp of life. The gift of the Spirit and the narrative character of Scripture indicate that the revelation of God is
ongoing rather than finished. The Christ event is pivotal to this
revelation, but is not exhaustive of God's ways with creation.[6]

In this view to respect Scripture is to recognise its historical
and contextual character. Terms such as heterosexuality and
homosexuality in the modern sense are anachronisms when
applied to scriptural texts. These modern descriptions attempt to
delineate a small minority of people who claim never to have
known anything other than same-sex orientation. Such a description could no more have been recognised by the biblical writers
than modern understandings of schizophrenia or paedophilia. In
short, what the biblical writers were condemning is not what
modern people are talking about when they speak of gays and
lesbians. Similarly protagonists of this interpretation are not

advocating promiscuity or seeking necessarily to subvert the normative character of heterosexual practice within marriage.

The challenge to the church is therefore to discern which of these two lines of argument is most consonant with the way Scripture indicates the character of God's ways with his pilgrim people who inhabit distinctive times and places and whose exploration of creation offers knowledge unavailable to the ancestors.[7] Crucially this means establishing a proper description of the term 'homosexuality', which is often assumed to be clear by all sides in the debate. Such discernment will need to attend to the way pertinent historic Christian practices, such as marriage, abstinence and celibacy, illuminate the ways of God in life as well as taking account of new insights in contemporary research. The issues cannot simply be foreclosed as if texts or self-consciousness exist in a vacuum. This means that theological arguments will both need to display accountability to the Scriptures while at the same time being part of the interpretative context for passages from these Scriptures. Thus the church as an interpretative community will also become involved. Given that the arguments on both sides are not conclusive, it may be that a measure of charitable difference will be required which recognises different responses within the same Christian tradition as has happened over the ordination of women to the priesthood. This is not necessarily a major problem, since the narrative character of Scripture indicates the contingency of human responses to God, which is but a reminder that we 'see but in a glass darkly'.[8] We don't always sing together in tune and Anglicans are part of the Elizabethan Settlement which sought to recognise this without fragmenting the church still further. What is essential is that the way of configuring this disagreement needs to be clarified before unilateral action is taken, in particular by churches in the west. The legacy of imperial history continues to render such unilateral actions the equivalent of 'might is white is right'.

Thus the role of the church as a varied community of communities needs to be acknowledged in the interpretation of Scripture, since Scripture cannot live unless there is a community which is reading it. Individualistic or idealistic readings are inadequate since the first fails to expose the social character of human identity, while the second denudes the Scriptures of their narrative and hence timeful character. Furthermore to be a sufficient community of interpreters the church must include those who call themselves gay or lesbian. In addition it will be important to attend to how and why existing Christian practices relating to sexual relationships, such as marriage, have emerged since these will be indicative of the church's understanding of sexual activity. Practices are less easily mutated into abstract ideas or timeless principles and, secondly, practices can be followed and examined to see what story or stories they tell.

For example, an examination of marriage as an English Christian practice over time would show that, while being predominantly a practice of stability devoted to keeping reproductive and property lines clear, latterly it has emerged as a more internally relational order. It still includes reproduction and property issues but is more attentive to the character and quality of the internal relationship of the couple. The difference between the marriage rite in the Book of Common Prayer and that of the 1980 Alternative Service Book is indicative of this. This is in marked contrast to the way marriage is understood in many non-western societies. In addition, with the advent of contraception this primarily relational rather than reproductive rationale for marriage has intensified further, given that most acts of sexual intercourse have intentionally been non-reproductive. Such sex has affinities with the non-reproductive sex of gays and lesbians. The fidelity and stability of marriage remain vital insights into human relationships. This mutation of the practice of marriage from a principally reproductive institution to a principally recreationally focused relationship within as well as beyond Christian practice might offer material help in grasping the way non-married relationships might be construed, particularly for those minorities, such as gays and lesbians, whose relationships cannot be expressed in marriage.[9]

Furthermore, the differences of practice and circumstance evident between the various cultures within which Christianity exists and engages in mission must also be part of the context for discussion. Struggles over circumcision and polygamy in Africa seem analogous to those involving gender and sexuality in Europe and North America. Interpreting the Scriptures means recognising the character of the interpreting communities and the relationship between the whole and the parts. Certainly in Anglican thinking this has not been sufficiently resolved. For example, Anglicans will need to determine whether ethical uniformity is possible across such vastly different communities or whether provinces are the appropriate unit for such uniform practice. In short, the Scriptures need the church to be faithfully and adequately interpreted. However, this process needs to be mindful of the Dutch Reformed Church's unilateral interpretation of Scripture in South Africa which gave legitimacy to apartheid.

Scripture and the common sermon

From the above I have tried to explore a 'common' reading of Scripture, that is, one which is a community enterprise attentive to tradition but alert to the way the Spirit is guiding us today. This does not avoid the challenges of engaging with the texts in depth. Simply assuming that the way we read the texts today is identical to the way they were understood at the time of their composition, or could be so, is to ignore the differences of time, place, culture and identity which the very origins, character and languages of Scripture set before us. Hence the challenge for an interpreting community is to read behind the text, on the text and in front of the text. Reading behind the text is a way of speaking about imagining the historical context of whatever part of Scripture is being read. Reading on the text is about discerning the literary style and character of the text. Reading in front of the text is discerning what sort of world the text opens up for us to see and where it directs our gaze. Such rich reading will enable the scriptural score to be faithfully sung or played.

However, as I have argued earlier, a further step needs to be taken and that is to recognise that the community reading the Scriptures is itself something of a text. It has its own context, its internal structure and it has a particular orientation or perspective on life, which needs to come to consciousness. In the interface of these two texts emerges something fresh, unique and mutually challenging. In particular it is fresh and challenging because, unlike a lot of reading, it is explicitly about the primary matter of life with God. Furthermore, these readings will themselves be provisional, since they are readings or singings which take place before all is clear; in Christian jargon, they are eschatologically relative.[10]

Oddly enough, this political reading of the Scriptures recovers the importance of the sermon as a contextual and authorised engagement with the story of the Scriptures in church. Often sermons have been regarded as incidental to the ongoing life of church. To some, they are not sufficiently academically polished. To others they are too anecdotal. To others they can appear too individualistic. However, properly conceived they represent arguably the richest form of theological reflection available. It is richest precisely because it is most political, that is, most intimately about how a particular community of Christians within the wider church is learning to follow God in the context they inhabit. As such a proper sermon is necessarily dialogical, since a sermon happens when a community listens for God together rather than simply the preacher as singular agent imposing a perspective upon them.

When I compare my roles as theological tutor and parish priest, I am convinced that the primary theological role was that of parish priest. It was the discipline of reflecting regularly upon the story of Scripture in and with the particular community of St Mary's, Doncaster, that most expressed what theology is about, namely following God's light in the particularities of life. The more academic theological task remains an important one since it represents an attempt to do this in conversation with the wisdom disciplines at their frontiers. I have no desire to diminish this vocation. However, academic theology is necessarily a minority and elitist exercise, which can distract attention from the primary theological task of nourishing Scripture's society, the 'ordinary' church. It is also prey to abstraction as its integration with the embodied church is not intrinsic to its approach.[11]

Hence if there is one role which modern clergy would do well to recover, it is that of the parson, the person called by the wider church to discern God's wisdom in particular contexts through prayer, reflection and conversation. This is represented in the Church of England's underestimated parochial structure. Of course there will need to be a more flexible understanding of the 'parochial' as relationships in society are less geographically determined than in the past, as we noted in Chapter 4. However, the underlying notion of commitment to context, which the parish and parson represent, is essential if the story of God in life's particularities is to be sung in appropriate melodies for the varied communities of the world. Thus the preacher as cantor occupies a pivotal role in this regard, which requires the most profound, yet simple, grasp of the contours of this story, a wisdom which can only come through the most disciplined of practices and conversation. For it is as particular communities of church live in the light of the epic of God, borne witness to in Scripture, that others will be challenged about the claims of this story upon them. Without this embodied apologetic, Scripture remains simply a collection of ancient texts for eccentric academics. With such embodied apologetics, Scripture comes to be seen as a classical display of the gracious wisdom, love and redemption of the God of Jesus Christ, whose life is active in analogous ways in the varieties of created existence today.

Summary

In this chapter I have tried to show how Scripture represents the heart of the plot of the great epic of God's engagement with creation. In textual form it represents the score of God's music, which the Christian community in its various contexts and times sings or plays, becoming thereby the music or embodiment of that story for their generation. This is by no means as simple as it sounds, since the interpretation involved in this demands the most attentive and disciplined of practices, practices centring on worship, prayer and service. I have given examples of where this sort of contextual discernment leads to tensions within the Christian community as well, inevitably, as beyond it. In the process I have tried to recover the primacy of the sermon as a theological reflection relative to other forms of theology. Likewise I have indicated the necessity of active belonging to a worshipping community if Scripture is truthfully and properly to be lived. I have also used the term 'the story of Scripture' not as a way of flattening out the diverse stories and styles of literature in the biblical texts, but because I believe that the story of Scripture comes as we wrestle with all these stories aware that their unity is held in the identity of God and pointed to in the bodies of Christians, whose lives claim to be unintelligible unless the way they are seeking to live finds coherence and destiny in the story Scripture reflects and is a part of, the epic of God's ways with life. In the next chapter I will attempt to explore the implications of this and the previous chapters for public ministry in the church and particularly the Church of England.

6 Marginal ministry

Licensed leadership

Anglicans have a tendency to like words. As a cleric of the Church of England I have a licence to minister. It reads:

> **WE, CYRIL GUY ASHTON, BISHOP SUFFRAGAN OF DONCASTER**, in right of **THE RIGHT REVEREND FATHER IN GOD JACK** by Divine Permission **LORD BISHOP OF SHEFFIELD** to our well beloved in Christ **JOHN BROMILOW THOMSON**, Clerk in Holy Orders, BA., MA., GREETING! WE DO by these presents GIVE AND GRANT to you our Licence and Authority to perform the Office of **Director of Ministry** for the Diocese of Sheffield in preaching the word of God and reading the common prayers and in performing all other Ecclesiastical Duties belonging to the said Office (you having first before Us taken such Oath and made and subscribed such Declaration as are by way of custom in such case required)AND WE DO by these Presents authorise you to receive and enjoy all and singular Stipends, Profits and Advantages whatsoever which from time to time may belong to the said Office IN WITNESS WHEREOF by the authority of an Instrument of Delegation made on 4th March 2000 by the said Lord Bishop of Sheffield under the provision of the Dioceses Measure of 1978 the Episcopal Seal of the said Lord Bishop of Sheffield is affixed to these presents and we have subscribed the same the second day of February Two thousand and one in the Second year of our Consecration.
>
> + Cyril Doncaster

This may seem a bit of a mouthful and the rhetoric can sound pompous, given the way language has mutated over the generations. However it is also worth pointing out the value of such language. In the first place such language reminds me, the recipient of the licence, that I am embedded in a story greater than my own. The licence, expressed in this way, disturbs the tyranny of the present so evident in contemporary western living, where history is simply another interest-group TV programme and what really matters is what I as an individual make of my own life. Similarly the licence is a disturbing reminder that I am webbed into identities and accountabilities which are not mine to control. Ministry, certainly as understood by Anglicans, is always derived and shared. It is never 'single seater service' and is always to be in conversation with others. In this sense it reflects the general orientation of Anglicans towards a conversational and collaborative witness to the grace of God, despite the sad contradictions that our history and contemporary practice display.[1]

I learned this importance of this in a very stressful way when I was left in charge of St Paul's Theological College, in South Africa, when the Principal was away at a conference in Zimbabwe. Some tensions had been brewing among the student body, which involved one of the black students. It was being alleged that he had inappropriately disciplined a child in his keeping and that this might involve more than simply discipline but could include child abuse. As the senior member of staff present I found myself facing a confrontational issue which, given the fragile condition of social life in South Africa at the time, could explode quite easily. I therefore asked the student whose child was involved to come and share his concerns with my other colleagues and me. This he declined to do. However, a caucus of the 'African' students did come to see me about this issue, representing this as a 'coloured' versus 'African' issue and one which was causing considerable tension in the black student body. Hence, since accusations were flying around, my other colleagues and I invited the 'accused' student to tell us his story in the presence of a doctor. This he did and it emerged that he had indeed disciplined the child but not in any way that could be construed as more than this. However, since the parents of the child were not willing to make any formal complaint, it was felt that the best way forward was for the accused student to apologise for any misunderstanding and to clear the air before the student body. This he did, apologising explicitly to the particular student around whose child the issue revolved.

Initially I could sense some tension in the atmosphere but naïvely assumed that such openness would close the matter and allow the community to resolve it. However, immediately after the meeting ended the student parent came over to me and released a tirade of abuse, verbally and publicly assaulting me for the way the proceedings had taken place. He then stormed out and did the same to a 'coloured' colleague, accusing him of colluding with white decision-making. Instead of the affair being resolved it was intensified, leading me to suspect that there was a power struggle within the black caucus of the student body. This was in part because the aggrieved student was a prime candidate for the role of elected Senior Student later in the year.

Looking back at this experience, I am aware that it could have been dealt with more easily if I had taken my licence more seriously. The complexities of the situation meant that I was inadequately equipped to resolve the issue. The child discipline problem was simply a presenting issue masking a more profound tension. In order to face this issue properly, a more senior figure was needed, since I, as a young white foreigner, was symbolically the wrong person to engage with the issues involved. I should have asked the Bishop, who lived locally and was chairman of the college council, to address the problem, immediately rather than afterwards. It was naïve of me to think that by emulating the approach of the Principal I would be sufficiently equipped and respected to do likewise. Instead, attention to the meaning of my licence would have enabled a more constructive engagement with the issues involved.

Licensed ministry is therefore about being braided or webbed into a community. It involves intrinsic belonging, accountability and protection. The licence not only 'allows', in the literal sense, but also limits what this particular officer of the Christian community can do as a public representative of the Anglican Church. I may have all sorts of particular theological interests, liturgical preferences and ideas about the ideal church. What this licence does is to require these to converse with the wider church.

Ministerial accountability to God is expressed in accountability to his people, represented for Anglicans in the personal oversight or episcope of the bishop. The bishop, for Anglicans, is the personal expression of the church as a whole with particular responsibility for a particular dimension of that church, the diocese. Hence accountability to the bishop is a way of speaking about their accountability to the universal church particularly manifest in this diocese.

Furthermore such accountability is a political accountability since the church, as a Christian society, represents a way of being in the world that involves questions of identity and practice which are social rather than simply individual. The licence is thus, intentionally, a protection in at least three ways. It protects the Christian community from unaccountable ministerial tyranny, it protects the Christian leader from isolated exposure to church and those beyond it and, in some way, it protects the latter from the dangers of charlatans posing as church leaders. As part of the Diocese of Sheffield with the memory of the 'Nine O'Clock' service in our history, the need to attend and respect what licensed ministry means remains a hard-learned lesson.

Nevertheless, when all this is said, as any Anglican cleric or lay minister will assert, the licence is actually a very generous one. Within its terms there is a great deal of room to explore the particular roles that the bishop licenses his officers to. This is why the image of a jazz-player is so apposite. Any jazz-player of merit is a competent practitioner of music but is also able to improvise. Furthermore jazz-playing is a social affair, with different artists contributing to the whole in a way which reflects their individual uniqueness but also the discipline of listening and responding to each other. Their togetherness is the premise for their improvisations rather than the latter being the means by which they produce a common sound. At a time when, within the Church of England, there are temptations among some to privilege individualistic views of ministry or interest-group agendas, the character of jazz-playing helps to illuminate the most profoundly Anglican understanding of the exercise of ministry in and through the church.

Creative ministry

Licensed ministry is therefore about flexibility and improvisation within a commitment to accountability and the character of the Anglican polity, present and past. In addition, since licensed ministry is not confined to ordained ministry, it allows for a considerable variety of potential expressions within the permission of the bishop. As an incumbent in the Church of England I was always amazed by how much more freedom I had to explore the call of God in the parish I served than I perceived ministers in other Christian traditions possessing. The freehold with its cure of souls was both awesome and yet also exhilarating. I was called to serve the church catholic, the church diocesan and the church parochial, and by parochial was not meant simply those who actively participated as congregation but anyone in the parish for whom St Mary's was the church of first resort. Such ministry takes time to flourish.

When we arrived from South Africa and moved into the vicarage I remember thinking that this parish would be our sphere of ministry for the best part of a decade, a form of marathon running rather than sprinting. Time was available to see people and prayers grow and materialise. Time was also available to enable relationships to be tested in the security of commitment. In South Yorkshire people summer and winter and then summer you again before they begin to trust you. They must be given time. Incumbency is about being committed to a people and a place for a serious period of time. It represents one of the more demanding and yet enriching of vocations and I have found that the way the Church of England envisages incumbency offers time and space for this. I certainly know that after three years as incumbent, when all my 'tricks' had been played, temptations to escape the frustrations of the parish were inhibited by the commitments implied in the freehold and cure of souls. It was as if I had to learn that God's time and mine were not necessarily synchronised and that people, like plants, need time to grow. Hothouses can be helpful in certain cases, but for resilient and stable growth, slower and more patient husbandry is required. Creative ministry depends upon commitment of time and person. Service has no shortcuts.

The parish of St Mary's Wheatley in Doncaster illustrates this challenge well. Historically it was a parish of two halves, the terraced owner-occupiers to the north of the main arterial road, Beckett Road, and the mixed, more substantial housing to the south. Broadly, one side of the road corresponded to traditional working-class culture, while the southern side represented the affluent middle classes. The church and vicarage were situated just on the south side and initially were roughly at the centre of the original parish which had been developed in the late nineteenth century from St George's, the main parish church of Doncaster. However, with the inter-war housing developments and then the post-war relocation of folk from the town centre to Wheatley Park, the parish church became more distant from the majority of people. Even when its 'daughter church', St Paul's, became an independent parish in 1992 just before I became incumbent, the location of St Mary's was towards the town-centre end of the parish. In addition, with the demise of domestic service, the rise of suburban living and the high cost of running large properties, quite a number became bed and breakfast hotels, homes for the elderly or multiple-occupancy dwellings. Within a generation, I estimated, the area had changed from being socially stable and respectable to being much more mixed, with a minority of dislocated and socially mobile temporary residents. In the train of this change arrived the familiar problems of inner urban areas as wider tendencies to social anonymity, along with the particular pressures the social changes brought, led to a sense that lower Wheatley was on the edge of respectability. At one time the local primary school was reserving 20 per cent of its nursery and reception places for 'bed and breakfast' children. People often commented to me, during my time as vicar, that the area had gone downhill and was not as it was. While aware that these voices represented contentious perspectives, there was a sense that longer-term residents were paying the cost of the social changes. Fecklessness was always pushing the frontiers in the form of drug pushing, drug abuse, theft, carelessness about the social fabric of the area and then, as a result of a change in police tactics, prostitution became a major issue in the streets around the church and vicarage.

What this meant for me as incumbent was that it took me

much longer than I expected to grasp the character and dynamics of the parish. Indeed, although I did the obvious thing upon arrival and searched out the census material, this was inadequate to the task. I had to visit and talk and walk the streets and listen. Initially when I arrived in the area I assumed that the church was failing to connect with people because of an image problem. Clergy represented the affluent social classes and the need therefore was to deconstruct this impression, true though it probably remained of me, by dressing more unpredictably and yet akin to the men of the area. I had my ear pierced as a way of symbolising this commitment and, to an extent, such an approach by the priest did open up all sorts of conversations. I remember asking a lad for a donation for Christian Aid when visiting a local street and, upon being refused, noticed that he too had an earring with a cross in it. I pointed this out to him and was able to ask why he wore the symbol but didn't support the cause! Similarly I found that my receding hairline meant that I could make a virtue out of a necessity and have a very short hair cut. This again disturbed stereotypes and offered occasion for engaging with local people in fruitful ways.

However, as I got to know the area I realised that I was in danger of misunderstanding the character of the people and the neighbourhood. Expectations about priests from the past had to be respected and connected to if one's own ministry was not simply to be a 'flash in the pan'. Creative ministry was about exploring the symbols rather than about discarding them. It was about enabling them to work in a way that opened up possibilities rather than closing them down. I therefore began to dress more evidently as a cleric and to appreciate the importance of this and of my robes for those who were not regular attenders of the church. Indeed I noticed that in this area people dressed up to come to church. Hence for the vicar to dress casually or to appear scruffy was to work against the expectation of the parishioners. It could easily be an imposition of a patronising view of people from another social order, rather than an attempt to engage creatively with the identities of those one was called to minister to. Furthermore, clerical symbols mattered particularly to those beyond the congregation. Removing them when visitors were present in an attempt to build bridges actually confused and diminished the expectations and understandings of these visitors. In addition this contributed to the invisibility of the church in society as its public servants became camouflaged and thereby hidden from view.

By attention to the particulars of this place, many of my assumptions about how to minister as incumbent were therefore challenged. Once again this took time as I had to learn how to understand the people and the place. It also required that I had to listen to the locals and recognise the vital role of the 'long stay' worshippers. I was the 'resident alien', whereas they were the 'old hands' with the depth knowledge of the traditions and practices of the parish.[2] To assume, as I had, that I could grasp the way ministry could happen in this parish simply by looking at good practice elsewhere and a number of theory books, was to misunderstand the character of the challenge, especially in a context of social mutation. In such a context the danger of losing symbolic connection is even more apparent. Hence reinhabiting symbols in a creative way became an imperative. Getting children to come into the church from local schools and being dressed up in clerical regalia became a vital mission strategy, yet all of this still meant seeking to represent the hospitality of God in the hospitality of the worshipping community towards any who would come.

Critical ministry

In all of the above, I was seeking to explore how to enable the congregation to represent its core identity as a gospel community more clearly. Dressing down was motivated by a desire to engage. The same motivation led me to dress up again. Yet as I struggled with the business of recovering and making connections with those who didn't come to church, the question which haunted me was 'Why should these folk bother with church if a hotline to God is all that is necessary for salvation?' I could not see, as I have mentioned earlier, why going to church should be so important beyond providing a context for rites of passage and other occasional social affairs to take place. It was only as my own dissatisfaction with this state of affairs combined with my reading around the project of Stanley Hauerwas, that I began to recognise the challenge of ministry facing me. Increasingly I saw that ministry in the sort of society England was becoming would involve equipping Christians with the resources critically to resist the powers that seek to rule human lives in place of God, while remaining hospitable, open and challenging to that society.

Such resistance and resourcing would require a much richer understanding of the place of church in discipleship. Congregations would need to become more distinctive and cohesive communities, open to the outsider, but nevertheless committed to a deepening quality of social discipleship. In my experience the parochial structure with its symbiotic relationship between congregation and parish as mission context enabled this to happen. Similarly the freedom and vocation of an incumbent represented the symbolic commitment to this. Co-operating with the Spirit of God and the wider church to form a distinctive hospitable community of devotion and mission was my calling as an incumbent.

In some way I believe St Mary's Wheatley was becoming this sort of community. It was unconsciously becoming a sort of local religious order serving a neighbourhood with the incumbent as 'abbot'. Visiting the parish became a shared ministry. Preparation for the sacraments became a shared ministry. Undertaking projects of various sorts became a shared ministry. My role was to encourage people to improvise where opportunities for ministry became apparent and to offer my own particular contributions as a complementary rather than a rival offering. We were in ministry and mission together and, although we represented different symbols, roles and responsibilities, these were to be of mutual support and encouragement rather than in competition.

Such an approach to ministry in and through being church is vital in a society such as ours where the resources to resist the totalising powers of late capitalism are very limited. Indeed most counter-culture challenges to these 'soft' but colonising powers are themselves parasitic upon the sort of social orders they critique. Arguably only communities which are rooted in traditioned, transcendent order have the possibilities to resist and to discipline the claims of such imperialism. The Christian community represents one such tradition and, in England, the historic Elizabethan Settlement still offers some resources which might suggest a future for the church and ministry, even though, as mentioned above, much has now eroded.

The intention of this Settlement was to conceive of the English nation as a Christian social order in two dimensions: the dimension of public worship and the dimension of secular living. Public ministry was itself, therefore, distinguished in its practice and accountability. The clergy were accountable for the ordering of public worship. The laity were accountable for the social order. Here was common worship in action. Both, clergy and laity, were ordered to seek for the wisdom of God in English society within different but complementary domains and united in a common conversational attention to God. This common conversation prevented either dimension from claiming total wisdom and power. It positioned all claims and activities of power within the horizon of God's love and judgement. It reminded everyone in society of the provisionality of what they represented and of the penultimacy of all human endeavours.

Sadly the failure of this settlement has seen the attempt, since the eighteenth-century Enlightenment, to divorce these two discernment domains. Indeed liberty has been construed not as seeking to serve God in a variety of social contexts, but as escaping the claims of public attention to the Christian, especially Anglican, narrative of this God's character. It has been an attempt to decouple 'secular' discernment from the moorings of public worship. In the process this 'freedom' has actually rendered people prey to powers which do not declare themselves, or regard themselves as penultimate or provisional. Hence, as in the case of the parable of the casting out of seven demons, our present state, though superficially more comfortable, is actually about a far more intense slavery. The liturgical listening of a Christian society has been marginalised, with the consequence that the resources immanent in such reflective attention are ignored and decisions about the political ordering of life become practical atheism.

Ministry today, however, cannot simply lament the loss of an earlier settlement, which itself was an attempt to resolve the legacy of the medieval church that emerged from the Con-stantinian settlement of the fourth century. Ministry today, though, can recover a number of resources within this history which may be pertinent to its contemporary form. For example, the notion that the church is a polity suggests that, as English society increasingly dissents from the Anglican settlement, so greater attention to the politics of Anglican living may need to take place. This need not imply a new form of clericalism, since Anglican polity is ordered by synods. It will mean, however, that synodical government will need to become much more suggestive of the character of Anglican discipleship.

Furthermore, licensed church ministers, lay and ordained, will need to attend to their political calling as ministers of Christian communities seeking to embody the Gospel in particular places and amidst particular communities. They will need to become organic theologians, that is, those embedded in various congregations called by the wider Christian community to help these communities listen for God in and through the practices of common worship and mission. Their prophetic task will therefore be about calling the Christian community to represent Christ, the prophetic sign of God, to the people and places they inhabit.

In Anglican terms this will be about exploring more emphatically and explicitly the distinctive Anglican stream of discipleship and would undoubtedly involve closer engagement with the international church. Likewise mission will have a more evangelistic disposition. While England cannot be equated with a pagan context, the conscious memory of Christian believing is so tenuous in society, that the notion of mission as return has to give way to mission as sharing good news in fresh ways. Ministry and mission will become more congruent. Ministers will have to be missioners. As noted above, my experience in Wheatley indicated to me that the parish, if it is to survive, will need to be regarded as a territory of mission. Within that territory will be gathered a worshipping community whose ministry will be exercised in ways consonant with the challenges of that place.

The above is effectively a scaling down of the possibilities of Anglican polity to a size more congruent with the embodied church of today. Of course there is a debate within Anglican thought about what it means to belong and there remains a challenge to encourage those who carry the mark of baptism to realise that baptism in their public devotional practices. However it is also true that that witness must be embodied if it is to be credible, particularly in a word-saturated and cynical world. Put bluntly, churches will only grow as the creative difference that Christ brings is more evident in ordinary yet diverse disciples' lives and, in particular, in the lives of Christian ministers. As a vicar in a low churchgoing area I found that the embodied Christian community grew and its financial condition became more stable because increasing numbers of people found the quality of God's life present in that community attractive and challenging. There was no magic wand about this. Nor was it about perfectionism. It was simply holiness, that is, reflecting the character of God by being faithful in the most basic of practices, such as hospitality, praying for people, visiting the sick, the lonely and the parish, giving to God and to the poor. Certainly as vicar. I sought to be imaginative, to take risks, to encourage and to challenge. However, this was only of help because the embodied community, warts and all, was committed to becoming more faithful. Liminal ministry needed the stability and support of a committed community, which was determined to listen and attend to God's call for the particular neighbourhood.

Playing in concert

Ministry in more distinctively holy congregations will not deny the past and the ongoing integration of church with society. Indeed I believe that Anglican ministry in particular will seek to represent church in new and fresh ways in order to continue its commitment to the people of England. Our ancestors' challenge remains a project to aspire to. However, public ministry in Anglican terms will need to become more varied in shape and relative to the mission challenges faced. For me as a vicar this meant my encouraging people to explore ministry of various sorts, and delegating responsibility to people. At diocesan and national levels imaginative initiatives involve looking again at the shape and configuration of public ministry, using partnerships, minster models of ministry, chaplaincies, schools, associate priests, wider oversight to experienced ministers and so on.

Indeed it is encouraging to note the way the Church of England in its recent report, *Formation for Ministry within a*

Learning Church, is moving in this sort of direction.[3] Furthermore there has been much creative work done on this area already along with issues of local and collaborative ministry.[4] What is imperative is that ministers are encouraged to be entrepreneurial, rather than repetitive, not simply technically proficient but possessing creative wisdom. This takes time, patience and courage. It cannot be gained by swift copying of abstract blueprints.

Conclusion

This chapter has sought to show that Anglican ministry is intrinsically contextual and thus accountable. Yet within this accountability there is remarkable flexibility and creative possibility. The latter depends upon the character of the gathered Christian community in a particular place, not as an independent body, but webbed into the greater story of the catholic church. In co-operating with the Spirit of God congregations can become creative and prophetic signs of Christ in the world. The discovery of this, however, cannot take place in the abstract, but only as ministers execute their service in and through the church. Ministry develops as good practice is shared, permission for adventure given and risk-taking encouraged. It is best expressed as common worship, mission and service, that is, clergy and laity together listening for God in particular contexts.

7 Marginal movement

Out of Africa

As a child brought up in Uganda I was aware of difference from an early age. This was my norm, so visits to England where whites were the majority and where, in the 60s and early 70s, minority ethnic and religious communities were less evident, were surprising. While the majority of Ugandans were Christians, there was a sizeable Islamic presence and we lived within sight of an Ishmaeli and a Sunni mosque. My parents employed a Kenyan Muslim man as cook and one of my early recollections was of discovering him weeping in our kitchen. On asking my mother why he was weeping she told me that his brother had been killed in a train accident and then tried to explain to me the different beliefs Christians and Muslims had about death and salvation. I was also fascinated that he had several wives. One of his sons, Onyango, was a playmate of mine and in the innocence of childhood the differences that we represented seemed to elide into the common joy of friendship.

Another vivid memory is of United Nations Day at the government primary school my siblings and I attended. Nakasero Primary School was a kaleidoscope of nationalities and colours, which came into full glory on this day when uniform was dispensed with and children were encouraged to dress in their national costume. As a Briton, despite some Scottish blood, I had nothing more interesting than 'normal' clothing. On this day I stood out as the boring one, precisely because the norm was British attire. The same could be said today for American gear.

However, despite this memory of ironic exclusion, my childhood formed me to appreciate and value the diversities of human existence. Furthermore, my parents were deeply influenced by what became known as the East African Revival and the Balokole (the 'saved ones') movement. At its best this renewal movement brought Africans and white expatriates to a place where they recognised that in God's community they were of equal worth. Indeed some of my parents' most moving stories were of local African people without formal education, sharing pearls of wisdom about the grace of God. I suspect my own commitment to discipleship for the ordinary is rooted here. Thus church as a community signifying the possibility of harmonious difference, and humanity as a rainbow community, were notions that were deeply embedded in my psyche. Of course being part of the privileged dimension of that reality only became apparent to me as I grew older. However, the love, patience and enthusiasm of my Ugandan friends and especially of the African Christians instilled in me a profound insight into the character of God's glory. In addition the way Ugandans had transcended the terrible bitterness of Christian–Muslim conflict in the late nineteenth century was also a lesson to me in mutual respect without capitulation.

It was this memory which drew me back to Africa as a young adult. Ironically it was to South Africa that I found myself being drawn, through friendship with Revd Fred Hendricks, who was doing further studies in Oxford at the time. We arranged a student exchange and I went across to South Africa for eight months and witnessed the terrible legacy of apartheid, the attempt to deal with difference by structural segregation. As mentioned above, I returned to lecture and teach at St Paul's College, the Anglican seminary, for three years after my first curacy at the time when the legal structure of apartheid was collapsing and formally being dismantled. However, law cannot unpick human formation and apartheid will take generations to exorcise from South Africa. Nevertheless, although South Africa and the Church of the Province exorcised any naïve romanticism I might have retained from my childhood about interracial or inter-religious relations, it also intensified my recognition that the only way for people of difference to live without destroying the image of God in each other was to accept the legitimate presence of each other as fellow creatures in a common world.

Such a heritage brought its own challenges when I was invited to become incumbent of St Mary's parish in Doncaster, an area of England with very few minority ethnic or religious communities. This seemed strange to me at the time. However, the challenge before me was how to use these experiences to help Christians with very little experience of pluralism negotiate the challenges of an increasingly pluralist society. One of the unexpected delights at St Mary's was to find overseas Christians working at the Doncaster Royal Infirmary coming to the church. Perhaps they felt that we shared some affinity with each other as a result of our respective histories. What it certainly did was enable English Christians to enjoy their difference, especially when we had international evenings, with world food to boot. It also gave confidence to some of the local Afro-Caribbean community to join us. Furthermore, it made it easier to introduce signing at some of our major services during the last two years of our time there when students and staff from the College for the Deaf, where my wife was employed, came to church.

Clarifying pluralism

My experience of a plural society in Africa was of an empirical reality. It was more about people and lives than about an ideology. Certainly in South Africa some Islamic radicals sought to identify Islam with a spurious historical purity, which contrasted with the legacy of Christianity in the continent. However, having visited the East African coast around Dar es Salaam and Mombasa, I was aware that Islam and Christianity both have their ambiguous pasts to deal with. The question facing the world and the churches was how to live with this empirical rather than ideological plurality of life.

Both my experience in Africa and as a parish priest in England have convinced me that two different ways of construing pluralism are often conflated. Pluralism as an ideology is often equated with pluralism as an empirical reality. Pluralism as an ideology implies that difference is the essential character of reality. Difference is how things are in life, whether it be in terms of religious belief, political conviction, economics, ethnic diversity or whatever. In this view any attempt to think in universal or absolute terms is doomed to failure since it conflicts with the way things are and should be. Universal resolution is not possible in this sort of world, marked as it is by finitude, perspective and, for many, imperfection or sin. It is a fantasy proposed by those seeking to dominate. The only reason that universal perspectives have been evident is not because they represent a truthful response to reality but because they represent an imperialist and pretentious power. Empires of any sort are an attempt to impose singularity and to force closure upon variety and difference.

According to this view all empires ultimately fail and display the inadequacy of their foundational convictions. Even the empire called 'modernity' is failing as protests against its presumption to have resolved the irreducible conflicts of the seventeenth-century wars of religion through the use of reason have gained strength. Whether it be western intellectuals, under the ambiguous rubric of postmodernism, or majority world communities rejecting the 'western' universalism of the colonial legacy, the contemporary intellectual atmosphere is to regard all claims to totality as pretensions to power and hence suspect. While it may be true that postmodernism represents the infantile regression of bourgeois university intellectuals whose role in late capitalist societies has been marginalised, it is certainly true that their co-operation with this fate has been aided by their eagerness to decry possibilities of resolution and the quest for truth within the Enlightenment project.[1]

As a vicar constantly engaging with the simplistic confidence which the legacy of the Enlightenment gave, especially to the opinion-forming classes both locally and through the media, I found the deconstructive critique of modernity very refreshing. However, the intuition of cosmic integration lying at the heart of the Enlightenment project, an intuition actually parasitic upon Christian believing and shared by all the major faiths, seemed to me to remain vital if the ideology of pluralism was not only to avoid becoming self-contradictory, but also was to offer more than hopeless chaos and the triumph of the fortunate. Unless there was some sense of a whole or a common destiny, of the possibility of truth, then there could be no future, no hope for the destitute and no possibility of calling the abusive to account. I found that people in my parish were postmodern only when it came to matters of pleasure, such as choices around homes, clothing, cars, leisure and so on. When it came to matters of suffering, or injustice, theft, prostitution, drug abuse, death and other traumas, they were far more likely to use the language of universal truth. Certainly such rhetoric could be qualified, but the intuition of integration, of justice, goodness and righteousness remained stubbornly resistant to the idea that the thief was simply inhabiting a parallel universe of meaning or that the pimp on the street had as much right to pursue his trade as the market-stall trader who was in the street-watch patrol.

In addition, and more ambiguously still, I found the arrival of the ubiquitous baseball cap during my incumbency a sobering reminder of the limits of postmodernism and its tendency to collude with the soft colonising of people by mass advertising and its promoters. The fact that in ten years a form of clothing which emerged from another part of the world and which was associated with a sport scarcely played in England achieved such universal presence indicated to me that the hidden character of modernity was alive and well. It had simply exchanged the ivory towers of the academy for the shopping malls where mass culture could be marketed more lucratively. I felt some sympathy for Indian and African radicals wondering how English clothing could have achieved such hegemony in alien climates intrinsically hostile to it.

Pastoral practice as well as intellectual wrestling led me to believe that pluralism as an ideology like postmodernity, its philosophical expression, is not only self-contradictory (that is, it makes a claim to totality in the very same breath as asserting that difference is the character of reality), but also crushes the most profound of intuitions which ordinary people hold dear. It represents the very pretension to power it rhetorically seeks to subvert since only the security and privileges of the university could spawn such an acidic critique whose consequences actually undermine the possibility of the university, let alone society, as a conversational community. It represents a demeaning of those without the intellectual tools to resist. It renders the poor even more vulnerable than when there was some agreement about norms to which they might either aspire or at least resort to when abused. It represents atheism in its most destructive form. It is the ideology of the intellectual aristocracy.

As the superficial attractions of postmodernism, the ideology of pluralism, became less appealing, I found myself trying to recover a way of life which recognised difference but did not lose the intuitive sense that such words as truth, wholeness and justice were meaningful. As a priest I also wanted to be part of a way of life which was not simply in thrall to the present and its fantasies about the future. The pastoral practice of listening to particular stories implied that identity and meaning required a sense of a whole. In particular, funerals represented a challenge to the notion that life was simply a series of dislocated individualistic impulses or choices. It was in funeral addresses that I found a resource to challenge the superficialities of postmodernism, since here was an attempt to give both shape and interpretation to an earthly life now concluded, but within the horizon of a greater story as yet unfinished, the epic of God's ways with his creation. Moral intuitions and narrative need among ordinary people questioned the adequacy of a way of construing life which refused to engage in criticism at the very moment when it criticised those traditions which were committed, however provisionally, to doing so.

It seemed to me that being an Anglican, in particular, was helpful in this attempt to explore the old tension between the 'one' and the 'many' without denying or destroying each of these poles. The Church of England, as mentioned earlier, emerged into its current shape under Elizabeth I as an attempt to hold together difference within a common sense of attention to the divine. It was a sort of ecumenical experiment configured around principled provisionality and a conversational grasping after truth. Complete resolution of differences and the achievement of absolute clarity had to be left to God. Nevertheless the practices of prayer and worship exposed the gathered community to the grace of God in distinctively formative ways. In addition the recitation of a cosmic narrative, whose character had been put to the test across different cultures and in different times, located this attention and its stories within a cosmic community of fellow travellers. In the ambiguity of life this did not imply moral superiority among worshippers. It did not imply a swift insight into the mystery of God in life. However, it did mean that the sense of the presence of the ultimate in the penultimate both gave assurance that the particulars of life mattered eternally and should not be crushed and yet also reminded those gathered that their perspectives were provisional and contextual.

Anglican worship and discipleship, at their best, could therefore accept wide variances and tolerate difference in a way that secular modernity and more 'closed' views of church could not. What secular modernity lost was a sense of its fundamental accountability to that which transcends the human and hence its own provisionality. It was therefore trapped within the limits of human perspective and doomed to confuse the particular and contingent with the universal and eternal. It forgot that the condition of being a creature is that we are within creation and hence cannot view the whole. We may feel our way towards the walls and roof of the house of creation, but we can never assume that our architectural insights adequately indicate the character of the house.

What Anglicanism at its best offered me as I reflected upon my formative years, my experience in South Africa and my time as a vicar in an English parish, was a humble yet committed truth-seeking community which sought not to destroy difference but to accept it as part of the provisionality of the created order which was as yet not wholly redeemed. In theological language Anglicanism represented 'eschatological reserve in practice'. Historically it was a response to empirical pluralism within the Christian tradition, but it is also suggestive of how this Christian church might suggest ways of responding to the new empirical plurality of contemporary England. It is also a way of believing which seeks to be open to the wisdom of God beyond its ecclesiastical contours and is attentive to the narrative character of identity. Its dynamic approach to truth-seeking, whereby worship comprises attention to the stories of Scripture, the stories of tradition and the stories of sound learning or reason, means that the present is always positioned by the past and yet open to the new. There is no sense that everything God is revealing is in our possession or control. We are still in a conversation.[2]

In terms of engaging with the empirical reality of pluralism (the presence of communities of difference within the same social or geographical space), this approach has the confidence to share its understanding of the truths about God and creation, while accepting that this understanding is provisional and hence able to be revised. Just as a person's life involves an ongoing telling of the story of their identity from the vantage point of a provisional moment, and the same person's funeral represents a closure of that earthly narrative and a vantage point which provides a more stable position from which to understand the person's earthly life, so the Anglican way of engaging with truth is to respect wisdom, the distillation of human experience, while taking account of the timeful and hence narrative character of human living with which God has graced us. This means that how we understand at any one time is narratively, but not definitively, given form. As we travel on, so the way the story is told changes, not in an occasionalistic sense, but in a way that draws its bearings from where the story has got to and hopes to travel. The fullest account of this story, however, awaits God's ending, the Parousia.

This means that issues which cannot be resolved in this world can have judgement suspended upon them in many cases. As has often been remarked, if my convictions are to be respected, then I must respect yours, even where we disagree, so long as we are not, in exercising such tolerance, acting in a way that abuses that tolerance. For theists, such as Anglicans, it is the accountability to God's final telling of our stories which acts as a check upon any flabby tolerance which fails to share its story courageously and truthfully. In this way there lies a path between the dangerous simplicities of Francis Fukuyama's 'The End of History' thesis, which has affinities with its rhetorical enemies Marxist-Leninism and Maoism, and the 'Clash of Civilisation' thesis of Stephen Huntingdon.[3] Without a transcendent accountability for the human community, there is no escape from either the totalitarianism of the former or the conflictual pluralism of the latter. The secular needs to return to its proper relationship to the worship of God if a plural society is to be a peaceable and respectful one. Without this it will simply become a policing ideology representing naked power rather than liberating space.

Ministry as conversation

From the above it can be seen that many responses to pluralism from within Christianity and from without have not proved adequate to the challenges facing ministry in the contemporary era within England. The exclusivist view, that the existing community of faith has possession of the total truth of God and can represent this in an immediate way, is undermined by the conflictual rhetoric evident between its most enthusiastic protagonists. Fundamentalism, the modern version of this tendency, is the most schismatic of all traditions. However, the opposite approach, the inclusivist one, is also wanting in much the same way as the postmodern pluralist ideology I have been criticising. It is itself contradictory and, furthermore, seeks to include all under a universal category called 'religion' without recognising that this category has been generated from within one tradition and may not be recognisable by other communities of faith, such as Islam. In short, religion is a Christian category. In addition this approach further underestimates the incommensurability of various truth claims. They cannot be dissolved into a common vision or language. Even the 'anonymous Christian' approach popularised by the Roman Catholic theologian, Karl Rahner, tends to patronise other faiths by diminishing their integrity. Both the exclusivist and the inclusivist neglect to attend to the intrinsic place of language in understanding and consequently the located and contextual character of all understanding. Both naïvely presume that all can be reduced into something without loss. They simplify the human condition and neglect the character of human identity.

A more plausible approach, as George Lindbeck has indicated, is to acknowledge the reality of incommensurability and the linguistic character of what are popularly known as different religions.[4] Just as French cannot be reduced to English, nor English to French, so no 'religious tradition' can be reduced to another or translated into a neutral third common tongue akin to Esperanto. Such an approach recognises that discerning truth requires participation in a community, which not only rhetorically speaks but actually lives a particular language. He calls this the cultural linguistic view. Each culturally linguistic view is tried and tested by its capacity to resolve the new challenges life presents and thereby to keep itself in business. However, there are difficulties here. The first is wrestling with how such distinctive communities can inhabit the same space without destroying each other. A second is that this approach renders each religion another self-sustaining commodity enclave.[5] A third is that it is also unclear where the boundaries are between distinctive traditions. For example, is secular humanism an ideology or just a fallback for sloppy thinking? To what extent is it parasitic and therefore part of Christian believing? Equally, the cultural linguistic view does not adequately explain how people are converted from one faith to another. It reduces truth-telling to a shouting match.

My own preference is for what Rowan Williams presents as the eschatological view. Indeed I think that this is a particularly Anglican way of dealing with pluralism within ourselves but also in society, and it has helped me to give theological form to the issues ministry has raised for me both in England and in Africa. The eschatological view assumes that all will be resolved, but by God, in God's good time, and that this is not yet. It refuses to identify our vision of God's ways with God's vision of God's ways. The fullness of God is always yet to be discovered. Hence, in the interim, we try to respect difference and gain as much coherence as we can, always recognising that we shall never achieve a total vision before the coming of our Lord. Provisionality is therefore built into this view, even though conviction of the truth-bearing character of Christian believing, for Christians, is not given up. Equally, toleration is not about seeking to accept all without judgement. It is about recognising that the respect I hope for from others will require that I also offer that respect to others. Furthermore eschatology implies that we do not seek for or equate a religious organisation with God's kingdom. The empty tomb in particular implies that we do not control Jesus. The world church is a contingent but indicative sign of heaven as a rainbow community. Anglican wisdom expressed in the interplay between Scripture, tradition and sound learning (reason) offers a flexible and open grasp of truth, which accepts the reality of plural perspectives within a worshipping community, yet is committed to testing and sifting these rigorously.

Ministry with integrity, therefore, involves recovering a number of responses to difference present in our tradition which may well have been forgotten, historically, as English Christianity has become comfortable with a position of dominance. Now that this is no longer the case attention needs to be given to analogous experiences of our ancestors in the faith, such as the Exilic period in the Old Testament and the pre-Constantinian church and also to our fellow Christians in the parts of the world where minority experience is the norm. This does not mean attempting to return to these eras. We can no more recover the innocence of the pre-Constantinian church than Uganda can pretend that the British Empire never happened. Nevertheless, the experience of independence in Africa is a sober reminder that the way we deal with the past and the insights we draw from it are vital if we are to move on. Similarly, the terrible legacy of apartheid in South Africa reminds Christians that, unless we keep in conversation with communities of faith which do not share our perspectives and hence blind spots, we shall be tempted to confuse truth-seeking with vested-interest defences.

With this in mind I would suggest that the following will help us minister with integrity in the sort of society which England now is and is likely to become. They have been forged in the experience of ministry in a variety of contexts and while by no means exhaustive, represent for me the implications of being a public representative of the Christian community. In the first instance, we need to recover the importance of the ear. In a culture which has emerged as the eye has achieved dominance, the ear is an underestimated organ.[6] The ear represents the importance of listening and the way listening prioritises the 'other' in a manner the eye can miss. The eye is always prone to confuse its vision with truth since it appears so immediate. In addition, seeing can suggest that we control the view. Listening or hearing, on the other hand, is always a response to that which engages us. Listening to those who are different to us reflects the challenge of all the great monotheistic religions. In each our principal task in life is to listen to and for God, who is other than, rather than simply an aspect of, ourselves. The Shema and the opening of the Fourth Gospel indicate this disposition. Indeed, it is as we listen that we learn to look well. This may be why, in the Fourth Gospel, key words which revolve around responses to the Word made flesh are the words for sight, looking, beholding, glancing and the like.

In the second place it is important to engage in conversation rather than rest content with silence. Silence can mean respect but it can mean a refusal to engage. The character of Christian believing is that we live in a conversational relationship with God. Hence ministry is about enabling that conversation to take place. Creation reminds us that we are webbed into all that exists and hence to be a creature is to be in a conversation of sorts. The character of a conversation is that it is open-ended, that is, we do not know for certain how it will end. It also presumes that we don't know everything. Otherwise we would not be in conversation. Conversation involves learning. Without conversations we simply dumb down. Equally, in interfaith conversations there is no conclusion given in advance since that would be to substitute abstract ideology for step-by-step agreements.

The third approach is to recall the challenge of Jesus to welcome and pay attention to the stranger. This was at the heart of Jesus' ministry because it is at the heart of God's relationship to creation. The stranger represents the one different to us. The Pharisees sought to establish a Jewish comfort zone beyond which strangers were kept. Rhetorically it was about equating God's hospitable space with a carefully delineated expression of the Torah. Jesus welcomed the latter into God's hospitable space, regarding God's reign as the intended implication of the Torah. This was to be a reign which, by reflecting the character of God, necessarily included invitations to those beyond the pale. Ministry is about going out and welcoming the stranger and not seeking to require that the stranger become one of us in advance or necessarily at all. As someone once said to me, it is about hosting, hearing and hallowing.

A fourth resource is to explore what it means to celebrate God as Trinity and to contemplate the perichoretic character of God, that is, the Christian conviction that God is not only an interplay and intercourse of persons, but that this reflects how God is with the created order. It is of the character of God that God infuses and inhabits all of reality and therefore is to be discerned in that reality. There are no 'no-go' zones for God. Hence the challenge is to discern the grace of God in other responses to the divine. Jesus isn't the container of all meanings but their judge. Incarnation means that Jesus is marking out the future for all people.[7]

The fifth insight for ministry is to encourage the sharing of stories rather than the dealing out of dogma. Anglicans particularly believe that we are in God's narrative world. Hence worship matters to us more than ideological certitude and everybody's story is necessary for the whole. This is why symbolism matters to us in our acts of worship. For example at the Chrism Service the interplay of the cross, the bishop, the Bible and *Common Worship* inform how the story is liturgically expressed. It is also why Anglicanism is often untidy and takes time to embrace change. Stories by their nature are particular and take time to hear.

Sixth, ministry needs to recover confidence in the integrity and capacity of the Christian story to do its work. In a pluralist society Christians are no more required to be silent than any one else. However, confidence isn't necessarily about noise-making. Rather it is about knowing who we are before God so that we are not threatened by difference and otherness. Equally it is about being prepared to unlearn things from the past. In this way we can be true to our story. Thus worshipping, living and teaching the faith is vital. Involved in this is the awareness, eschatologically, that we are not complete. Hence we need others in order to become the rainbow universal community to which we are travelling and of which, at present, we can only be a sign. The church is not a tribe to trump others. Our story of creation is about a God who rejects totalitarianism, since he creates that which is different to himself and yet is intrinsically relational (we are, therefore I am).[8] Nevertheless, we can present our claims to inhabiting a truthful story of God when there is evidence in our signature that a tentative rainbow is emerging. This happens when our churches reflect the conviction that this story of God has space for all and can resolve the tension between the one and the many. It happens when there is an embodied apologetic represented in a community which embraces the differences of race, time, gender and context joyfully and without destruction.

Pluralism and partnership in action in Darnall, Sheffield

A creative example of partnership in action has been developed in Darnall, Sheffield by Revd Canon Mike Fudger and Imam Mohammad Ishmael. In conversation with them it is clear that a key element in establishing this partnership has been learning the importance of listening before critiquing each other's faiths. Similarly, having some knowledge of each other's faith has been vital in building trust. Mohammad Ishmael's background included attending Bible College and studying Christian theology and biblical studies in Pakistan prior to coming to Britain. He had also been an Imam in Cardiff, a prison chaplain, a schools inspector, a further education lecturer and is Secretary of the Council of Mosques. Similarly Mike Fudger was the first Anglican priest to engage with Muslim theologians at a conference in England as well as being regarded by the Muslim community in Darnall as a proper parish priest, that is, a priest who is seen and known by all sections of the community including the Muslims.

Darnall is a plural context with a 25 per cent minority ethnic population which itself includes religious communities of considerable ethnic diversity. In the Muslim community there are Yemenis, Somalis, Pakistanis and others. Tensions exist in and between communities as well as their shared common concerns about drug abuse and crime. In this environment the key question for Mike Fudger is 'Who are the church's allies?' The Muslims, with their devotional life, have practical affinities with Christians and hence become friends in the divine gaze. To begin to work together means not seeking in the first instance doctrinal agreement but identifying common sympathies and priorities. Part of the ministerial task in this environment involves interpreting what is going on across boundaries. For example, issues of dress, eating traditions and gender roles in schools represent such boundary situations, which Mike Fudger's friendships with Muslims enable him to interpret and assist with. This reflects what it means to be a parish priest, that is, a priest to the parish, including the Muslim and other religious and ethnic communities.

For Mohammad Ishmael the role of the priest of any faith is about reminding people who we are before God, and of our destiny with God. Thus it is to guide people in the name of God and hence to walk closely with people. This involves challenging stereotypes, for example notions of the sort of 'jobs' ethnic and religious minorities might be expected to hold. It is also about affirming that we are citizens together in this society. Certainly there is also a need to share faith, and indeed Muslims learn about Jesus from their earliest years via the Qu'ran, in contrast to the relative ignorance of Christians about Mohammad. Such isolation needs to be broken down.

In the practice of this 'partnership learning' about the 'other', incremental trust is built up through conversation and shared engagement with community issues. There is no sense here of confessional capitulation or an unwillingness to share respective faiths. Such learning happens in a number of ways, first through the partnership offering an embodied expression of social and religious diversity in contrast with the more mono-ethnic areas of Sheffield. This reinforces the work of the World Development Education Centre and the churches of the Abbeydale Road corridor in south-west Sheffield and is especially important after 11 September 2001.

Second, such partnership begins to offer Christians more insight into Islam, and especially Jesus in Islamic perspective. As Mohammad Ishmael pointed out, in Islam Jesus is seen as a holy prophet who will return at the end of time to judge the world as Messiah. In the Qu'ran he is referred to 71 times and while the question of his death divides Muslims and Christians, they share convictions about his virgin birth and his role as a light of God (cf. Suras 5:46 and 19:30–1). Mohammad also noted that within Christianity there is pluralism in terms of how Jesus is understood. This should enable Christians and Muslims to respect their different ways of looking at Jesus, the light from God. In addition he noted that the common Abrahamic ancestry of Christianity, Judaism and Islam meant that these faiths were relatives rather than strangers. Hence they should stick together, especially when media and politicians misrepresented them. He himself had been influenced in his views about a possible war with Iraq after hearing Archbishop Rowan Williams' viewpoint.

Third, the perception of Islamic resistance to change can be addressed. Mohammad pointed out that just as Christianity had to be flexible in different contexts, so Islam was also changing in certain areas. For example Friday sermons are now translated into English, not only given in Arabic. The way forward is respectful integration rather than isolation, which eventually leads to disintegration. Friendship is the bridge as Christians and Muslims share the same social space.

Fourth, the fragmentary tendencies of Islam and Christianity under the pressures of modernity can be compared and contrasted. Mohammad argued that Islam has produced far fewer heterodox movements in modernity than either Christianity or Judaism, although there are analogous heterodox traditions in

Islam, such as those of Sufis, Ishmaelis, Druze and others. However, the basics of Islam are more commonly agreed upon, thereby enabling greater internal coherence to the faith.

Conclusion

This chapter has attempted to explore how ministry can be exercised with integrity in a pluralist context. By pluralism I mean the presence of communities of difference rather than an ideology which seeks to police what is acceptable belief and practice. In the process I have tried to indicate that openness to the stranger enables Christians to witness without denying their character. Indeed it is by reaching out to engage the stranger in conversation that Christians reflect most closely the ministry and mission of Jesus. Such reaching out in friendship, such conversation, is evident in the way Mike Fudger and Mohammad Ishmael have begun to work together. Their friendship is about mutual respect, many shared convictions and a willingness to recognise that their loyalty to God enables them to keep going in their differences, since God is their common Lord.

Eschatological reserve and hope prevent any attempt to foreclose difference. They also orientate Christians by indicating that our common destiny of sharing in the kaleidoscopic symphony of God's glory in the great finale of creation illuminates our hope and practice in the present. However, ministry is correlative to the communities represented. Hence the politics of the Christian community must represent this hospitality, attention, respect and sharing in tangible practices. It is these which will not only enable friendship to happen, but will give others beyond the Christian community a taste of the character of Christian truth claims. For Anglicans, in particular, this would seem consonant with our faith pedigree. Hence, as the next chapter explores, the formation of Christian ministers is of vital importance.

8 Marginal training

If, as I have been suggesting, the challenge of being church today in England involves exploring what it means to be marginal to much of what is perceived to be significant and relevant, then those called to public ministry, ordained or lay, will need to be formed with this as the norm. One of the concerns I have already noted is of clergy who emerge from large, 'successful', often suburban churches and find that they are deployed in parishes where the possibilities of recapitulating the models of church they have been formed in are simply not there. This can lead to a retreat to suburbia or a student church, or in some cases to leaving public ministry altogether. I recognise the struggle here, having served as a curate in a relatively large and thriving suburban church. Indeed I sometimes say, tongue in cheek, that to get from west Sheffield to inner urban Doncaster I had to go via South Africa, such was the contextual change. Nevertheless, as the character of congregational ministry changes and as stipendiary ministry in the Church of England is put under increasing pressure, the way ministers are trained for this liminal role becomes crucial. Indeed the affinities with training for overseas mission becomes apparent, not only in terms of cultural awareness learning but predominantly in terms of survival and flourishing in an apparent desert. To aid this we need to explore a particular sort of 'web-based' training, that is, training contextually. Contextual, meaning 'woven or webbed together', implies that training for ministry involves training with and within the web of the church.

Learning survival skills

If the public ministers of the church in England are to survive creatively in marginal mode, their education needs to be of a kind that instils confidence in the character of their calling, encourages collaboration, flexibility, improvisation and risk-taking. It should also involve drinking richly at the wells of Scripture and tradition and giving attention to the wisdom of the Christian community represented in its people, memory and openness to God at work in the world. As I have already intimated, ministry-training developments in the Church of England are encouraging, particularly in the move to regional training partnerships and to mixed-mode training. While I do not want to repeat the substance of the proposals, it does seem to me that the regionalisation of training for public ministry allows contextual nuances and variations to be explored in practical terms, a considerable improvement on present possibilities, especially in South Yorkshire. Similarly, mixed-mode training allows for a greater variety of students to explore vocational training without losing formative dimensions of the experience, and also allows for more flexible possibilities for when licensed ministry can begin.

However, while structures, pathways and outcomes are important, and much creative work has been done on this, my own contention is that the character of the training and its horizon remain of fundamental concern. This book reflects upon what it might mean to be a church often consigned to the margins. Nevertheless to be a church in the catacombs, as it were, is not to imply that what that church represents or bears witness to is really marginal or insignificant; quite the reverse.[1] Hence those who bear public office in this catacomb church will need to be even more confident in what they bear witness to than their ancestors to whom society showed greater deference. In what follows I want to suggest ways of exploring theological education and training which, I believe, would assist in appropriate ministerial formation for a liminal church.

In the first instance, biblical studies would benefit from becoming more embedded in congregational life. If, as I have suggested, the reading and studying of Scripture is a political activity (since it necessarily involves participation in the community which recognises these texts as Scripture and whose way of life forms people to read them truthfully), then approaches to studying the Bible will need to take account of this. Studying Scripture will need to include participation in a congregation rather than being learned abstractly as an intellectual exercise. This may well involve extending the collaborative approach to study to include within the training experience folk from particular congregations.

In this process the student and tutor will also develop communication and conversational skills vital if creative ministry is to happen. Furthermore, lectionary reading will be particularly important as a way of ensuring that the narrative shape of Scripture is preserved from the corrosive individualism of private judgement. It will also prepare trainees for the discipline of the Ministry of the Word week by week.

Church history, in particular, should be seen as the distinctive way the church remembers the past, rather than merely representing a dimension of that past. Such a way of reading history as church will also be a bulwark against postmodern tendencies to deny the possibility of history, and enable ministers to keep their moorings amid the anarchic individualism and presentism which are colonising much of the church. It will also help ministers to set in perspective contemporary challenges and to have recourse to analogous situations from which wisdom can be gained. Similarly, as narrative, this history will contribute to the eschatological orientation of ministry since narrative is intrinsically future-focused and is shaped and understood relative to its expected ending. The character of the ending Christians received from the teaching of Jesus is of God's vindication and glorious reign, a hope which gives perspective to the present.

Christian ethics in my view is better understood as theology since it represents an exploration of how Christians are formed to see and act in life before God, rather than giving abstract guidance on how to resolve abstract problems. In this sense what has traditionally been called doctrine or systematics will be included in the challenging of living within the Christian ethos rather than being a separate discipline. Theology is a way of being in the world rather than a reflection upon other primary approaches to existence such as sociology or philosophy. Doctrines are those agreements made within and across churches about the character of that theology. In this sense they are like grammar, as Lindbeck suggests, and theology is the language which helps us to see the way to live ethically. Thus theological ethics will need to equip ministers with the capacity to see how to live before God in diverse contexts. It will therefore be an ongoing and contingent exposition of the living and contemporary memory of Jesus carried in the church. It will certainly not offer them an abstract moral handbook. In addition the liturgical disciplines, which teach ministers how to pray and lead worship, become particularly vital as subversive acts challenging over-confidence in human agency on the one hand, and on the other refusing to despair in the face of sin and evil.

Pastoral theology will be about learning how to connect the wisdom of God, represented by the teaching of Jesus and its theological implications, with the particular stories told by those seeking guidance. It will be more like spiritual direction than about applying counselling techniques to clients and will be congregationally as well as individually focused. Training for this will best be a form of apprenticeship rather than simply an engagement with texts since, like the wisdom of a craft, this is not about technical expertise so much as about *phronesis*, the wisdom of a practitioner. Such wisdom is aware of the history and traditions of its craft but is also keenly aware that each congregation, person and situation is particular and not merely an example of a type. The mediation of wisdom under such challenging conditions demands skilled practitioners, people patiently schooled in the practices of ministry. Those being inducted into ministry will need to see their preparation within this horizon.

Missiology will be about learning to recognise the mission of God to redeem and restore all things in Christ. This is best discovered congregationally, since the gathered Christian community is properly configured to this end. Mission and evangelism will therefore be about community activity rather than being left to representative individuals. In Anglican terms, priesthood belongs within the church and hence the mission and evangelistic tasks of the church are community tasks within which the priest serves. When confronting parish visiting I realised that even a parish of six thousand people with over two thousand dwellings would mean that I, as incumbent, could never hope to visit every home. However if between fifty and sixty members of the congregation shared the visiting with me, then every home could be contacted in the parish within one afternoon. This indeed happened when we gave every household a Millennium gift. Similarly, visiting teams, congregational involvement in Christian Aid events, support for homeless people, holiday clubs for local children, and involvement overseas were examples of this community mission and evangelism.

Training in the web

Given what I have argued above it will come as no surprise that I am in favour of more congregational participation in the formation and ongoing training of public ministers of the church. Otherwise imaginary churches shape training, or particular congregations become benchmarks against which everything else is measured. This engenders an approach to ministry which is about recapitulation rather than about distinctive cultivation. Training in conscious conversation with contemporary churches both within and beyond the immediate context, including overseas churches, enables students to appreciate how the practices of these churches exhibit important theological truths which can easily be overlooked if abstract learning is the norm. For example, a congregation situated in an urban priority area, such as our neighbour St Paul's Wheatley Park, displays the nature of the Gospel as faithful social witness and service by its presence in the area. This stands counter to the 'success and effectiveness' preoccupations of much contemporary culture. In addition, the variety of stories present in the lives of this non-selective community offer rich resources for theological reflection about the nature of grace and the eschatological destiny anticipated in the Eucharist. Furthermore, regular Sunday worship itself can be seen as a major political challenge to contemporary society, proclaiming the primacy of God above all other political loyalties. Liturgical worship and the importance of lectionary scripture reading represent both nourishment for worship and the generation of correlative Christian identity. This challenges the notion that the Scriptures are like any other text, transparent to anyone independent of context, training and participation in the church.

Such a church is what makes sense of theology, for the lives of its members are indicative of what theology is about. In consequence this relocates the place of theological resource and reflection. These are not primarily in books of theology, important though they may be. Neither are they most evident in gatherings of like-minded Christians, encouraging as those can be on occasion. Rather, the resources for theological reflection and ministerial formation are found embodied in the practices of ordinary, often marginal, churches exploring what it means to worship the God of Jesus Christ today in their particular contexts.

I therefore agree with Stanley Hauerwas when he argues that the liturgical shape of Christian worship should act as a theological-ethical education syllabus. In an essay entitled 'The liturgical shape of the Christian life: teaching Christian ethics as worship' he illustrates this approach, reiterating the significance of the 'political character of worship as extremely important in order that worship not become "aesthetics" in the modern sense'.[2] He also rejects any 'and' between theology (and) worship, correlating worship, holiness and truthful vision/living. From reflection upon the liturgy he finds a call to look backwards through time, since theology is a tradition-determined craft, but also outward, since theology is about response rather than construction in the first instance. The structure of worship opens up eschatological questions, apologetic strategies, theological language, issues of evil, sin, confession, the way Scripture should be read and interpreted, issues of initiation, sustenance, ethics as ethos, atonement and mission. Such theological reflection upon liturgical practices enables learners to see what they are reflecting about and to recognise not only its appropriate relevance but also the essential place of the tangible and historic worshipping community in their ongoing learning as theological craftswomen and craftsmen. They are not learning a series of ideas as beliefs but are engaging in practices which indicate a way of worshipping, witnessing and serving in God's kingdom in contemporary contexts.

Such reflection will equip them with the resources to discriminate about how discipleship engages with those who do not yet know or worship the Trinity. This will form ministers, lay and ordained, who are committed to a conversational, collaborative, communal approach to discerning theological truth and exercising ministry in contrast to the expert and individualistic tendencies evident in some quarters. It will engender a proper humility and sense of symbiotic, if occasionally argumentative, friendship between ordained ministers and the congregation, as both are essential for the church's witness. It will enable boundaries of proper Christian behaviour to be discerned as worship forms holy disciples. It will provide resources to look again at practices such as marriage and having children, whose increasingly radical character in contemporary western society is underrated by Christians and non-Christians alike. It will help Christians gain a distinctive purchase on concepts such as justice, freedom, autonomy and rights. It will re-centre the dialogical sermon as vital to the practice of common worship. It will impart in churches an awareness of participating in a glorious epic. It will form ministers to be ecclesial improvisers, akin to jazz-players rather than being liturgical technicians or ecclesiastical archaeologists.

Ministerial character

Given the paradox that the truth of God's ways with the world is especially witnessed to by those congregations on the margins, ministerial character emerges as of vital significance. Precisely because the margins are not where many people in our society locate serious and challenging truth, the temptation to sit light on issues of ministerial character and formation needs to be guarded against. The representative role of the minister is more than simply a dramatic one. It is a vital symbol infused with the character of what it means to be a public minister in the church. In Anglican terms this is what is meant by priestly formation. Without serious attention to this the vocation of the minister will be vulnerable. For example, ordination is about the church ordering some to be its 'community people'. Hence who and what the ordained are is correlative to what the church is to be, that is, a holy witness to God's presence in the world. This role, therefore, is not to be derived from some extraneous or idealistic view of being a professional, or from notions of technical competence, or from the idea of the expert. Instead it is to be derived from the church as a holy people. By the quality of their lives and in their prophetic challenge the ordained are simply called to remind the church of its identity and calling.

Since the definitive prophetic sign is Jesus, it is by attending to how Jesus is and has been with his church and world that the cleric is given insight into the sort of character he or she should be manifesting. Indeed, to recover the proper calling of the priest or cleric primarily requires the cultivation of virtues rather than competencies, virtues such as courage, patience and hope. These reflect deep formative experience rather than simply intellectual awareness or repetitive technique, and depend upon the formative discipline of participating in Christian communities which, for example, visit the sick and welcome the stranger. Furthermore, this attention to the character of the minister recognises the lifelong pilgrimage that ministerial development entails. What is often called Initial Ministerial Training is simply a part, anticipated by much discipleship training and continued as further discipleship and ministerial development throughout life's journey. While such learning will involve the further acquisition of skills and competencies, its primary purpose is to develop the virtues and wisdoms which deepen the character of the minister and enable ministry to be vital and properly responsive. In the public ministry of the church competency and character belong together. However, while the latter can survive even if the former is not ideal, competency is no substitute for character formation.

Learning in new ways[3]

From the preceding discussion it is clear that distance and web-based/e-learning have to be employed carefully in the formation of Christian ministers. As a supplement and complement to the primary task of character formation, such approaches can be very creative. Indeed web-based learning has some distinct advantages when it comes to learning as a group, since more people can engage in on-line discussions than real-time seminars and the absence of face-to-face encounters can help some students to express themselves more fully. Flexibility of time and place are also assets of both web-based and distance learning approaches in that they allow responsibility for managing learning to rest with the learner, which is particularly appropriate for adults. However, there are questions which need to be addressed when considering either or both of these approaches in preparing candidates for public ministry in the church and for those already so engaged. The following are some of my concerns.

To what extent can virtual communities escape the narcissistic tendencies of the web? Does disembodied learning offer genuine or deceptive levels of disclosure and sharing? Is the challenge of the 'other' lost in such mediated encounter? Will video-conferencing escape this problem? Does e-learning privilege the powerful and exclude the poor and the elderly, or is the level of access sufficient for representative participation rates, especially if the learning community is an international one? Does web-based/e-learning, like distance learning, require an element of face-to-face encounter to complement, enrich and test its educational character? Will web-based learning reach learners who would otherwise be deterred from participating in an embodied community in the first instance, but whose confidence might be won as a first step towards discipleship? Do chat-room facilities allow more people to participate in and retain record of the learning experience or is this simply a multiplication of rhetoric with little genuine transformation? Are bodies intrinsic to theological education, or is a more docetic approach compatible with discipleship and ministerial formation? What are the implications of putting the learner at the centre if ministry is about being inducted into a community's craft?

Essentially the questions are the relationship between politics and learning and the nature of the politics essential to this learning. Certainly I would claim that we need to encourage a more adventurous and imaginative exploration of the sort of learning experiences we wish ministers to be theologically formed in. However, it is vital that they see themselves as learning and developing a community's craft, as opposed to a theoretical exercise of the singular mind or the banking of abstract information. It is also imperative that they gain a clear sense of their identity as servants within and of the Christian community. This is a particular challenge with distance and internet-mediated learning. Parodies of Christian community can be engaged in, as Graham Ward notes in *Cities of God*, unless such learning includes being part of tangible face-to-face communities.[4] The body, either as church or as person, must not be lost in learning, especially for the sort of leadership required by the Christian polity.

Training explorers

When I was involved in Initial Ministerial Education in South Africa I always struggled with the incongruity of the seminary. As the ministers of the Church of the Province of Southern Africa came increasingly from the black communities, an English training scheme seemed far removed from the ministerial realities in townships and rural areas. I often felt this tension when training people to preach and then listening to township or village preaching by indigenous people. Almost everything we were attempting in the college counteracted the traditions of communication in these cultures. Similarly, the analytical approach to theology and Bible, so webbed into the western psyche, received considerable critique from both African theology and Black theology. Indeed one of my reasons for not applying to become part of the staff of the new College of the Transfiguration was that I was convinced that it must be staffed, imagined and formed by those whose identity was primarily rooted in that context, rather than in western Europe.

In returning to South Yorkshire I found many of the same debates taking place among those involved in theological education and training in this part of England. What was happening was a recognition that 'single-seater' training in relatively abstract environments was not preparing people adequately for the challenges of ministry in this sort of environment. Certainly placements do help, such as the one we have in the Diocese of Sheffield whereby ordinands from Ripon College, Cuddesdon, Oxford, spend three to six months on the Manor Estate in Sheffield. However, even here there has been perplexity among some students when theology does not mean a discourse on Karl Barth or John Milbank, the incarnation or Christology, but about what it means for Christians to become part of the residents' association, or how listening to the local community's story about its past might relate to the Arian controversy (i.e., God with us). Ministers who can survive and even flourish in these situations need careful training and ongoing support in ways appropriate to the contexts in which they are to be servants. Indeed if the church is to reverse the tide of churchgoing decline, more imaginative ministerial outcomes need to be considered, with greater attention, at the outset of the vocational process, to possible ministry dispositions and outcomes and, in the experience of training, to the acquisition of practical theological reasoning.[5] Training for and in these forms of ministry should actively involve reflection upon the actual practices of the church in particular areas.

What therefore we need are imaginative and engaged theological educators who can form ministers for the challenges we face. I would suggest that the church today requires 'entrepreneurial ministry', that is, adventurous explorers serving in and with a section of Christian society, whose politics are about worshipping the Trinity, nourishing Christian identity, and mission. Such a role is intrinsically collaborative, conversational, contextual and necessarily about embodiment. It is learned through apprenticeship to other wise practitioners, other ministers and other disciples. Furthermore it recognises that the rainbow character of the church bears witness to the eschatological destiny of creation where all will be integrated into the magnificent complexity of the glory of God.[6]

Conclusion

The future for Christianity in western contexts lies, I believe, in a recovery of what it means to be embodied church. As one with an evangelical pedigree, I am increasingly convinced that the wisdom, stabilities, imaginative resources and accountabilities of the church through and across time and space are vital for our flourishing and engaging with the challenges we face. It is essential, as even evangelicals have become increasingly aware of late, to be consciously church and thereby be equipped with the skills necessary to discern God's vitality in the ambiguities of life. Hence these explorations of a 'catholic' evangelical and my hope that the church will cease to be on the edge of evangelical identity.

However, in recovering such a vision and its resources I also believe that we must come to terms with being a church on the edge of our contemporary society in a way which English Anglicans have not known. This does not mean defaulting on our historic responsibilities, but it does mean acknowledging that the shaping of our society is no longer relative to its Christian heritage in the way it seemed in the past. Nevertheless there are advantages to be gained from this identity. A church on the edge, I have argued, is a more alive and trusting church than one secure in its central position in society. To be on the edge is to recognise one's vulnerability and that the resources for life are always about risk. To be on the edge is also to see that where we are does not guarantee where we shall end up. Hence living on the edge requires new skills, fresh attention to our core virtues and a character which relishes adventure. To be a church on the edge of our society is also to be a church which has to recover its core sense of who it is and why it is here. Without this the edge will be a place of threat and anxiety, prompting a reactionary and desperate attempt to recover a more central location. If I have any criticism of some church-growth proposals, it is that they seem to be so preoccupied with growing something that they do not ask what it is that should be growing. It is as if growth of any sort is acceptable, whereas my own view is that the sort of growth that is required depends upon ensuring that the emerging congregation is indeed a faithful expression of the church. Being on the edge sharpens our awareness of what sort of 'plant' we are becoming and invites us to pray that God will give the growth that will enable us to flourish on the edge.

I believe that the sorts of communities of faith we need to become will be those characterised by a greater attention to what is distinctive about practising Christian discipleship and ministry in our sort of society, without closing our ears to the voice of God in the wider community. This will be about recovering confidence in the descriptive power of our language, our way of interpreting the ways of God with creation. It will be about recognising the vital and formative character of worshipping God-with-us in Jesus. It will be about following this Jesus around the margins of our society and finding, even in its centre, other edges on which we need to share the Gospel. It will mean inhabiting the story of God, which Jesus illustrated most intensely, of which a church on the edge is a sign. It will involve discerning how more adventurous ways of expressing ministry can be encouraged in order to serve with passion on the margins. It will mean reappraising our sense of power and significance in the sort of society we are now a part of. It will require that training for discipleship and for ministry become more flexible, challenging and collaborative than in the past, In short, to be a church on edge is to recognise that our calling today is to recover the adventure of being a holy church in the ordinary details of life, church which is not primarily about ideas but about bodies whose character, virtues and quality of life are inexplicable unless the Jesus we speak of is risen.

Notes

Chapter 1: Feeling edgy

1. John B. Thomson, *The Ecclesiology of Stanley Hauerwas: A Christian Theology of Liberation* (Aldershot: Ashgate, 2003).
2. Stanley Hauerwas, *Unleashing the Scriptures: Freeing the Bible from Captivity to America* (Nashville, TN: Abingdon Press, 1993).
3. The story of Abram and Lot is found in Genesis chapter 13.

Chapter 2: Marginal speech

1. John Milbank, *Theology and Social Theory: Beyond Secular Reason* (Oxford: Blackwell, 1990), pp. 9–12.
2. Paul Field and Stephen Deal, *Hopes and Dreams: A New Musical for a New Millennium* (Eastbourne: Kingsway, 1999).
3. John Milbank, 'The theological critique of philosophy in Harnann and Jacobi' in John Milbank, Catherine Pickstock and Graham Ward (eds), *Radical Orthodoxy* (London: Routledge, 1999), pp. 21–30.
4. Paul Avis, *Anglicanism and the Christian Church: Theological Resources in Historical Perspective* (Edinburgh: T. & T. Clark, 1989), pp. 8–10, 60–2, 290; 'What is Anglicanism?' in S. W. Sykes and J. Booty (eds), *The Study of Anglicanism* (London: SPCK, 1998), p. 415.

Chapter 3: Marginal worship

1. What follows represents a challenge to the conclusions of many of the contributors to a recent symposium which looked at the future of Christian practice in the next fifty years. Perhaps this represents a critical distance between those who practise church and those who speculate about it. See Grace Davie, Paul Heelas and Linda Woodhead (eds), *Predicting Religion: Christian, Secular and Alternative Futures* (Aldershot: Ashgate, 2003).
2. See Grace Davie, *Religion in Britain since 1945* (Oxford: Oxford University Press, 1994) and *Religion in Modern Europe: A Memory Mutates* (Oxford: Oxford University Press, 2000).
3. S. W. Sykes, 'Introduction: Why authority?' in Stephen W. Sykes (ed.), *Authority in the Anglican Communion: Essays Presented to Bishop John Howe* (Toronto: Anglican Book Centre, 1987), pp. 18–20. See also Stephen Sykes, *Unashamed Anglicanism* (London: Darton, Longman & Todd, 1995), pp. xviii, 111.

4. Daniel Hardy, *God's Ways with the World: Thinking and Practising Christian Faith* (Edinburgh: T. & T. Clark, 1996), pp. 251–2.

Chapter 4: Marginal mission

1. Brad J. Kallenberg, *Ethics as Grammar: Changing the Postmodern Subject* (Notre Dame IN: University of Notre Dame Press, 2001), p. 156.
2. See Ronald F. Thiemann, *Revelation as Theology: The Gospel as Narrated Promise* (Notre Dame, IN: University of Notre Dame Press, 1985), pp. 99–116, 148; John Webster, *Barth's Ethics of Reconciliation* (Cambridge: Cambridge University Press, 1995), pp. 2–7; and David F. Demson, *Hans Frei and Karl Barth: Different Ways of Reading Scripture* (Cambridge: Eerdmans, 1997), p. 9.
3. Ascetic comes from the root of the Greek verb *askeo* meaning to train or exert oneself.
4. In particular the work of Revd George Lings at the Sheffield Centre for Church Planting, which is based in the Wilson Carlile College of Evangelism in Sheffield, is an important resource.
5. Interestingly enough this census indicated that South Yorkshire was both confessionally Christian and above the national average at 75 per cent as opposed to 72 per cent. To an extent this may be due to the relatively small size of other major faith communities. It may also reflect the views of those who filled in the forms, who would be likely to use the Christian box more than any other in this region. However, even so this does raise questions about the equation of secularism with unbelief, as Grace Davie and others have noted.
6. Information about the Discerning Church Vocation project can be obtained by contacting The Archdeacon of Doncaster, Church House, 95–99 Effingham Street, Rotherham, S65 1BL.
7. For a discussion of this irony see Helen Cameron, 'The decline of the Church of England as a local membership organisation: predicting the nature of civil society in 2050' in Grace Davie, Paul Heelas and Linda Woodhead (eds), *Predicting Religion: Christian, Secular and Alternative Futures* (Aldershot: Ashgate, 2003), pp. 109–19.
8. For the roots of this idea see Stanley Hauerwas, *A Community of Character: Toward a Constructive Christian Social Ethic*, 4th edn (Notre Dame, IN: University of Notre Dame Press, 1986), p. 9.

Chapter 5: Marginal story

1. For a fascinating discussion of the self as the 'singing self' see David Ford, *Self and Salvation: Being Transformed* (Cambridge: Cambridge University Press, 1999), pp. 107–31.
2. Jürgen Moltmann, *The Church in the Power of the Spirit* (London: SCM Press, 1977), p. 35.
3. See Stanley Hauerwas 'The insufficiency of Scripture: why discipleship is

required' in Stanley Hauerwas, *Unleashing the Scriptures: Freeing the Bible from Captivity to America* (Nashville, TN: Abingdon Press, 1993), pp. 47–62.

4. While liberation theology is primarily associated with Latin America and hence, superficially outside the west, its categories and dispositions still originate in western ways of thinking which can be traced back through Marx to Kant. This does not reduce their challenge, but it does give them a sociological address. While much African theology is similarly dependent, my interest at this point was in listening for what was not western. For a discussion on theology in South Africa see my 'Modern Christian Thought, South Africa' in Alistair McGrath, *Blackwell's Encyclopedia of Modern Theology* (Oxford: Blackwell, 1993).

5. A helpful expression of traditional Anglican thinking here is in Peter Walker and Andrew Goddard, *True Union in the Body? A Contribution to the Discussion within the Anglican Communion concerning the Public Blessing of Same-Sex Relationships* (Cambridge: Grove Booklets, 2003).

6. For a distillation of this approach see Gareth Moore OP, *A Question of Truth: Christianity and Homosexuality* (London: Continuum, 2003).

7. For a conversation between various perspectives on Christianity and same-sex relationships see Timothy Bradshaw (ed.), *The Way Forward? Christian Voices on Homosexuality and the Church* (London: Hodder & Stoughton, 1997).

8. 1 Corinthians 13:12.

9. This argument is indebted to a paper by Stanley Hauerwas entitled 'Resisting capitalism: on marriage and homosexuality' in Stanley Hauerwas, *A Better Hope: Resources for a Church Confronting Capitalism, Democracy and Postmodernity* (Grand Rapids, MI: Brazos Press, 2000), pp. 47–51. It should be pointed out that this approach is not accepted by the rejectionist view of contraception held by the Roman Catholic Church. This view entails an absolute correlation between sexual activity and procreation, a correlation which implies the essentially reproductive character of marriage and equally rejects any forms of non-reproductive sexual activity. Thus homosexual intercourse is anathema, just as is heterosexual intercourse which inhibits potential conception.

10. Eschatology is the study of the end or goal, the Eschaton, of God's creative-redemptive mission and involves interpreting life within the horizon of this destiny.

11. A way of configuring this is to contrast two Greek words for wisdom, *phronesis* and *sophia*. The first refers to the wisdom of a practitioner, akin to a craftsman or a craftswoman, whereas the second refers to the wisdom of the scholar. The wisdom of the sermon reflects that of the practitioner and is arguably the primordial theology, since *sophia* theology is parasitic upon it.

Chapter 6: **Marginal ministry**

1. For the root meaning of contextual as webbing or braiding together see Daniel Hardy, 'The future of theology in a complex world' in *God's Ways with the World: Thinking and Practising Christian Faith* (Edinburgh: T. & T. Clark, 1996), pp. 32–3.
2. For the pedigree of this phrase see Stanley Hauerwas and William H. Willimon, *Resident Aliens: Life in the Christian Colony* (Nashville, TN: Abingdon Press, 1989).
3. *Formation for Ministry within a Learning Church: The Report of the Working Party on the Structure and Funding of Ordination Training* (London: Ministry Division, 2003).
4. See the work of Robin Greenwood, *Transforming Church: Liberating Structure for Ministry* (London: SPCK, 2002); Eddie Gibbs and Ian Coffrey, *Church Next: Quantum Changes in Christian Ministry* (Leicester: IVP, 2001); and Steven Croft, *Transforming Christian Communities: Re-imagining the Church for the 21st Century* (London: Darton, Longman & Todd, 2002).

Chapter 7: **Marginal movement**

1. Stanley Hauerwas, 'The Christian difference: or, surviving post-modernism' in Stanley Hauerwas, *A Better Hope: Resources for a Church Confronting Capitalism, Democracy and Postmodernity* (Grand Rapids, MI: Brazos Press, 2000), pp. 35–46. For critical engagements with postmodernity see also Anthony C. Thiselton, *Interpreting God and the Postmodern Self* (Edinburgh: T. & T. Clark, 1995), and Miroslav Volf, *Exclusion and Embrace: A Theological Exploration of Identity, Otherness, and Reconciliation* (Nashville, TN: Abingdon Press, 1996).
2. For helpful discussions of Anglican identity, particularly in English history, see Paul Avis, *Anglicanism and the Christian Church: Theological Resources in Historical Perspective* (Edinburgh: T. & T. Clark, 1989); *The Anglican Understanding of the Church: An Introduction* (London: SPCK, 2000); and *Church, State and Establishment* (London: SPCK, 2001). See also S. W. Sykes and J. Booty (eds), *The Study of Anglicanism* (London: SPCK, 1998); Stephen Sykes, *Unashamed Anglicanism* (London: Darton, Longman & Todd, 1995); and Stephen W. Sykes (ed.), *Authority in the Anglican Communion: Essays Presented to Bishop John Howe* (Toronto: Anglican Book Centre, 1987).
3. Francis Fukuyama, *The End of History and the Last Man* (Harmondsworth: Penguin, 1992); and Samuel R. Huntingdon, *The Clash of Civilizations and the Remaking of World Order* (London: Touchstone, 1998).
4. George A. Lindbeck, *The Nature of Doctrine: Religion in a Post Liberal Age* (Philadelphia: Westminster Press, 1984), pp. 16–25.
5. Rowan Williams, *On Christian Theology* (Oxford: Blackwell, 2000), p. 36.
6. Hans-Georg Gadamer, *Truth and Method*, 2nd edn (London: Sheed & Ward, 1993), p. 462.

7. Ibid., p. 94.
8. Ibid., p. 105.

Chapter 8: **Marginal training**
1. Oliver O'Donovan, *The Desire of the Nations: Rediscovering the Roots of Political Theology* (Cambridge: Cambridge University Press, 1996), p. 216.
2. 'The liturgical shape of the Christian Church: teaching Christian ethics as worship' in Stanley Hauerwas, *In Good Company: The Church as Polis* (Notre Dame, IN: University of Notre Dame Press, 1997), pp. 153–68.
3. I discuss these issues in conversation with the ecclesiology of Stanley Hauerwas in 'Training political leaders: theological education, ministerial formation and the ecclesiology of Stanley Hauerwas' in *The British Journal of Theological Education* 14.1 (July 2003), 46–7.
4. Graham Ward, *Cities of God* (London: Routledge, 2000), pp. 244–60.
5. For a creative approach see Bob Jackson, *Hope for the Church: Contemporary Strategies for Growth* (London: Church House Publishing, 2002). Practical theological reasoning should not be confused with putting theological ideas into action. Practical theological reasoning is a wisdom rather than a technique. It is about being formed into a practitioner who can recognise the theological issues embedded in the details of life and understands how to enable the Christian community in that place to respond.
6. The phrase 'magnificent complexity' comes from Daniel Hardy's essay 'A magnicent complexity: letting God be God in church, society and creation' in David Ford and Dennis L. Stamps (eds), *Essentials of Christian Community: Essays for Daniel Hardy* (Edinburgh: T. & T. Clark, 1996), pp. 307–56.

Select bibliography

Avis, Paul, *Anglicanism and the Christian Church: Theological Resources in Historical Perspective*, Edinburgh: T. & T. Clark, 1989.

'What is Anglicanism?' in S. W. Sykes and J. Booty, *The Study of Anglicanism*, London: SPCK, 1998.

The Anglican Understanding of the Church: An Introduction, London: SPCK, 2000.

Church, State and Establishment, London: SPCK, 2001.

Bradshaw, Timothy (ed.), *The Way Forward? Christian Voices on Homosexuality and the Church*, London: Hodder & Stoughton, 1997.

Croft, Steven, *Transforming Christian Communities: Re-imagining the Church for the 21st Century*, London: Darton, Longman & Todd, 2002.

Davie, Grace, *Religion in Britain since 1945: Believing without Belonging*, Oxford: Oxford University Press, 1994.

Religion in Modern Europe: A Memory Mutates, Oxford: Oxford University Press, 2000.

Davie, Grace, Heelas, Paul and Woodhead, Linda (eds), *Predicting Religion: Christian, Secular and Alternative Futures*, Aldershot: Ashgate, 2003.

Demson, David E., *Hans Frei and Karl Barth: Different Ways of Reading Scripture*, Grand Rapids, MI: Eerdmans, 1997.

Ford, David, *Self and Salvation: Being Transformed*, Cambridge: Cambridge University Press, 1999.

Ford, David and Stamps, Dennis L. (eds), *Essentials of Christian Community: Essays for Daniel Hardy*, Edinburgh: T. & T. Clark, 1996.

Gadamer, Hans-Georg, *Truth and Method*, 2nd edn, London: Sheed & Ward, 1993.

Gibbs, Eddie and Coffrey, Ian, *Church Next: Quantum Changes in Christian Ministry*, Leicester: IVP, 2001.

Greenwood, Robin, *Transforming Church: Liberating Structure for Ministry*, London: SPCK, 2002.

Hardy, Daniel W., *God's Ways with the World*, Edinburgh: T. & T. Clark, 1996.

Hauerwas, Stanley, *A Community of Character: Toward a Constructive Christian Social Ethic*, 4th edn, Notre Dame, IN: University of Notre Dame Press, 1986.

Unleashing the Scripture: Freeing the Bible from Captivity to America, Nashville, TN: Abingdon Press, 1993.

In Good Company: The Church as Polis, Notre Dame, IN: University of Notre Dame Press, 1995.

A Better Hope: Resources for a Church Confronting Capitalism, Democracy and Postmodernity, Michigan, MI: Brazos Press, 2000.

Hauerwas, Stanley, and Willimon, William H., *Resident Aliens: Life in the Christian Colony*, Nashville, TN: Abingdon Press, 1989.

Jackson, Bob, *Hope for the Church: Contemporary Strategies for Growth*, London: Church House Publishing, 2002.

Kallenberg, Brad J., *Ethics as Grammar: Changing the Postmodern Subject*, Notre Dame IN: University of Notre Dame Press, 2001.

Leech, Kenneth, *The Sky Is Red: Discerning the Signs of the Times*, London: Darton, Longman & Todd, 1997.

Lindbeck, George A., *The Nature of Doctrine: Religion in a Post Liberal Age*, Philadelphia: Westminster Press, 1984.

MacIntyre, Alasdair, *After Virtue*, London: Duckworth, 1985.

Whose Justice, Whose Rationality?, London: Duckworth, 1988.

McGrath, Alister E., *The Future of Christianity*, Oxford: Blackwell, 2002.

Milbank, John, *Theology and Social Theory: Beyond Secular Reason*, Oxford: Blackwell, 1990.

Milbank, John, Pickstock, Catherine and Ward, Graham (eds), *Radical Orthodoxy: A New Theology*, London and New York: Routledge, 1999.

Moltmann, Jürgen, *The Church in the Power of the Spirit*, London: SCM Press, 1977.

Moody, Christopher, *Eccentric Ministry: Pastoral Care and Leadership in the Parish*, London: Darton, Longman & Todd, 1992.

Moore OP, Gareth, *A Question of Truth: Christianity and Homosexuality*, London: Continuum, 2003.

Moynagh, Michael, *Changing World Changing Church*, London: Monarch Books, 1998.

O'Donovan, Oliver, *The Desire of the Nations: Rediscovering the Roots of Political Theology*, Cambridge: Cambridge University Press, 1996.

Percy, Martyn, *Power and the Church: Ecclesiology in an Age of Transition*, London: Cassell, 1998.

Robinson, John A. T., *On Being the Church in the World*, London: A. R. Mowbray, 1977.

Sykes, Stephen W. (ed.), *Authority in the Anglican Communion: Essays Presented to Bishop John Howe*, Toronto: Anglican Book Centre, 1987.

Sykes, Stephen, *Unashamed Anglicanism*, London: Darton, Longman & Todd, 1995.

Sykes, S. W. and Booty, J. (eds), *The Study of Anglicanism*, London: SPCK, 1998.

Stibbe, Mark, *O Brave New Church: Rescuing the Addictive Culture*, London: Darton, Longman & Todd, 1995.

Thiemann, Ronald F., *Revelation as Theology: The Gospel as Narrated Promise*, Notre Dame IN: University of Notre Dame Press, 1985.

Thiselton, Anthony C., *Interpreting God and the Postmodern Self*, Edinburgh: T. & T. Clark, 1995.

Thomson, John B., *The Ecclesiology of Stanley Hauerwas: A Christian Theology of Liberation*, Aldershot: Ashgate, 2003.

Volf, Miroslav, *Exclusion and Embrace: A Theological Exploration of Identity, Otherness, and Reconciliation*, Nashville TN: Abingdon Press, 1996.

Walker, Peter and Goddard, Andrew, *True Union in the Body? A Contribution to the Discussion within the Anglican Communion concerning the Public Blessing of Same-Sex Relationships*, Cambridge: Grove Booklets, 2003.

Ward, Graham, *Cities of God*, London: Routledge, 2000.

Warren, Robert, *Being Human, Being Church: Spirituality and Mission in the Local Church*, London: Marshall Pickering, 1995.

Webster, John, *Barth's Ethics of Reconciliation*, Cambridge: Cambridge University Press, 1995.

Williams, Rowan, *On Christian Theology*, Oxford: Blackwell, 2000.

Formation for Ministry within a Learning Church: The Report of the Working Party on the Structure and Funding of Ordination Training, London: Church House Publishing, 2003.

Index